Man Cover

Rev. Dr. Angela M. Battle

Man Cover
Copyright © 2018 by Rev. Dr. Angela Battle

Desakajo Publishing
Wilmington, DE
267-779-1475

All rights reserved. No part of this book may be reproduced or transmitted in any form or by any means without written permission from the author.

Printed in USA

Man Cover!

While based on a true story and all incidents are actual, this book reveals some of the struggles of a talented, educated African American woman in the corporate workforce dealing with institutional racism. There is a fundamental disconnect today in the corporation between the civil rights advocacy and the reality facing those of us in the new racial undercaste system for African Americans and other people of color (minority) are not being promoted in this particular company. Moreover, there is a new twist to the social injustice. We need to look at the ethics of who is allowed to have access to Homeland Security technology and its impact on human rights. Decisions are being made by people in power and position who have racist bias and or are a racist. While this is a federal policy matter, the sinister consequence of not addressing the economic injustice issue that has been carefully engineered by a selected few is largely responsible along with the fact of invading privacy of African Americans and other people of color. This creates an environment in which it is reasonable to ask how something akin to a racial caste system can exist in the year 2018. You can help by sharing this information and raising awareness on social media, the news and with your public officials to enforce the law and protect human rights and privacy.

Disclaimer

Because this book reveals the daunting truth about a select few individuals in power and position that oversees technology, you will see that they have intentionally placed typos, margins displacements and other grammatical errors. Furthermore, I deliberately took the time to ensure that the culprits' names, company and associates were not used. However, because of the sick demented plan of trying to block the truth they are willing to have place a name as an excuse to block this book from being publicly released. This is done to also flex their technical abuse of illegal use of power. However, the first question that will need to be asked is do you have the technical capability to change the names in her book. Question number two, did you change the names, company and or associations in her book. The beauty is the truth will still be revealed. I plan to rewrite this book after the trial to include the more detailed events and share references. Today, it is a cry for federal intervention into this matter.

Dedication

This book is dedicated to my beloved brother Wali Sharif whose life was snatched too soon and sacrificed for mine. He is the unsung hero. His life was taken because he was an African American male that had a sister who spoke Truth to Power concerning institutional and structural racism.

Table of Contents

Chapter One The Unsuspected 11
   The Coaching Session 14
   The Performance Evaluation 2011 17
   The May 2011 Equal Employment Opportunity & Human Resources Meetings... 18
   The Employee Assistance Program (EAP) Grab & Go... 19
   The Father Document of 2012 23
   The Company Police Reports................................ 23
   The Truth from the Grave 28

Chapter Two Without A Shadow of Doubt................ 31
   The Equal Employment Complaints 31
   The Company and Local Police Reports 32
   The Discovery 32
   The Lynching 33
   The Performance Appraisal Appeal 34
   The Letters Written to Authorities 35
   The Court 37
   The Draft 39

Chapter Three The Unveiling 41
   The Central Nervous System and Communication Cell Towers 42
   The Human Sacrifice for Science Experiment 48
   The Technology 50
   The Traffic and Bus Abuses 53
   The Personal Abuses 55
   The Work Abuses 58
   The Children Abuses 61

  The Biological Warfare Medical Technology Abuses 79
Chapter Four No Justice 83
  Further Abuses 87
  More Work Abuses 89
  Further Personal Abuses 91
  The Threats 92
  The Sexual Innuendos 100
  The Invasion of Privacy 106
Chapter Five Economic Injustice 107
  Work Related Economic Abuses 111
  Personal Loss Related Economic Abuses 113
  Family Loss Related Economic Abuses 117
  Ministry Loss Related Economic Abuses 118
  The Cruel and Heartless 124
Chapter Six No Boundaries and No Limits 139
  Passageville Patrol 142
  Virginia/Dallas Trip 143
  Car Towed and Ticketed 145
  Racial Profiled and Police Stopped 148
  Attempted Murder 149
  Money Laundering 149
Chapter Seven No Exit Plan 151
  Institutional Racism and The Structure 151
  The PACK 155
  The Grinch That Stole Christmas 155
  The Runaround and the Stall 158
   Physical Evidence Not Investigated 159
  The Unanswered Ethical Questions (Constitutional

and Human Rights Denied) 160
My Recommendation 164
My Plea For Federal Intervention 165
Specific Federal Necessities 170
Acknowledgements 174
Endnotes 175

Chapter One

The Unsuspected

*"Beneath the rule of men entirely great,
The pen is mightier than the sword. Behold
The arch-enchanter's wand — itself a nothing,
But taking sorcery from the master-hand
To paralyze the Caesars, and to strike
The loud earth breathless! Take away the sword,
States can be saved without it!"*

Macready, William Charles (1875).[i]

Today is Thursday and I sit looking out the window being gifted I can see some things the way they shall be and therefore enjoy them in a more beautiful way. Some say I have an optimistic view on life. However, in living my secure optimistic life, evil broke in and disrupted the peace and harmony. By evil, I mean blatant disregard of corporate policy, state and federal laws and human rights.

While I should not think that strange because that is what evil does! What is strange is a corporation that allows it. Walk with me as I share my story. Because of the hell I have gone through this is deemed as Satan's experiment. African Americans thought the Tuskegee Experiments were a travesty and they were. These new technological experiments considered in some realms are far worst. With the University medical research advances in chemical warfare, and access to the body via the spinal cord nervous systems and the electricity we carry there are all sorts of detrimental ethical medical problems.

It is common knowledge that Science has now found a way to mimic the human cell structure with cell towers. From your brain and down your spinal cord is the Central Nervous System

(CNS). Signals can travel along the spinal cord between the brain and the rest of the body. The spinal cord is the fiber cable or conduit. This can be done in split seconds as with all reflexes. With everything being computerized this technology can be used in humans, cars, and bridges to name a few.

How do you process the conversion from a cell tower to a human cell? Both human and computers give off electrical signals. Human signals are interpreted by our Central Nervous System. We have nerve cells that communicate with each other. A computer can tap in, receive, and interrupt that signal in both humans and computers because of our central nervous system. This is explained in more detail in Chapter Three.

Remember this is all done for two reasons; one racism, and two capitalism all at African Americans expense. This stems from their belief that the select few I reference in this book have entitlement and we are just property. Yes, even in this day and age we have some who viewed other human beings as property and their lives dispensable.

The fact that I am protected under the Conscientious Employee Protection Act (CEPA) has not stopped the disparity in the treatment, the discriminatory practices, and hostile environment in the work place. I even filed eight written and signed EEO complaints Equal Employment Opportunity Office. One included the fact that I was being followed to the restroom by my former supervisor. This was another complaint unanswered and not mentioned in court.

Every EEO complaint had excerpts of corporate policy and referenced corporate policy the corporate policy that they had violated. None of this was allowed to be submitted as evidence. Every year as employees you are sent a letter home stating The Company has Zero Tolerance for discrimination while there are countless reports, complaints and lawsuit of discrimination against The Company every year for this very issue. The policy is not read let alone enforced. It is a computer-generated letter that is sent out every year. The truth is they have Zero Tolerance for when you report the incident and so it is never addressed. Again, this was another item not submitted as evidence in my court case.

While the evidence was undeniable and accumulating in front of their faces, justice was denied. Despite the evilness, I am a living witness. While I am a living witness I also survive one of their illegal tactics which was how to discredit a good witness. What do you do when the plaintiff is an ordained Reverend and a Doctor as a witness? The witness is a pastor of a church, an author, a facilitator, a mother, a grandmother and an active member of the community who is well liked by her colleagues and family. You have to discredit her. So, you set the plan in motion with her being unsuspecting. You start with tampering with my work product after all I received commendable, outstanding and frequently exceed annual work reviews. I have been at The Company at this time for over ten years. I was recommended for promotion and had my paperwork put in the process. While my paperwork was conveniently lost a white female coworker name Gail paperwork submitted at the same time mine was went through and Gail received her promotion in a few weeks with pay. They had asked Gail not to say anything to anyone. Gail was under the impression that I too received my promotion and she stated to me jokingly it is a shame they asked us not to tell anyone.

When I filed my EEO case, human resources recommended that I be given the promotion and the pay back to the date that my coworker received her promotion and raise. Instead, the senior director said no. When I spoke with Human Resources they stated they can only recommend that it is up to the senior director to make the final decision. This is structural racism in action. Why would the person who has done the racist act be allowed to make the final decision?

While the challenge will be tough to fight, you nick pick, you give unclear directions in work assignments, and you change meetings on the calendar at the last minute. You delete crucial work needed to complete deadlines. Then you try to pick fights and place employees against each other. When this fails, you have to elevate your diabolical plan. You train others and the one that needs the new information you leave out. You then reprimand me for not knowing information that was never given to me. You praise one employee in front of another and insult, correct, and embarrass the other employee in front of each other. You upgrade the computer system and give me outdated antiquated equipment. You deny training. You take files from the desk. Hmmm! She still prevails because she knows her job, understands the system, and has faith in a supreme being. Again, this evidence is ruled not acceptable in court because the decision was already made before going to court. If the complaint is a hostile workplace, why not show a hostile work place.

The Coaching Sessions

The intensity tightened. The next step was the so-called force Coaching Session 2010 which is the new design name for Performance Improvement Plan. If I have an EEO complaint, why would I want that person to so-call coach me? Again, another racial tactic used. I fought Human Resources on this demand. I researched what a real work coach was, the selection process of a coach, and the qualifications to be a coach which my former supervisor did not meet. A coach is supposed to be someone you respect, trust and believe you can learn from him or her. I was told I had to meet or I would be written up which proves my point. It was not a coaching session as it was forced.

They would have a pre-meeting with the senior director, director and human resources and decide their plan of action. The Plan of Action is to overburden me with unrealistic work assignments and impossible deadlines. The system is designed for you to fail. They would speak positive at the initial meeting stating they have faith in you obtaining these so-called goals which were unrealistic while all the while waiting for you to fail. I had to come in early and stay late, and come in on the weekends to stay on top of the workload. The tasks that were supposed to be the secretary became mine. I went from being an administrator to filing, typing labels, and logging in data. This was one of their highlights of trying to stress me out as I was earning my second Master's degree in seminary at the time.

They were quite adamant about these coaching sessions and having them every week. What they did in these five coaching sessions was tried to switch my principal accountability with that of the secretary. I understand now they were trying to build their case to have me fired. Yet again, I messed up their plan. I stayed late, came in early, and worked on the weekends. Moreover, for the sessions he would send me demeaning emails and only bring my response to the meeting to show that I was not a nice person. Being the professional that I was I also brought the full email chain to the meeting showing how he attacked my work, me and my response was me defending myself against his false accusations. At this time, because of being overworked, not being able to take lunch, and being escorted to the restrooms, it did cause me to gain excessive weight as I stayed more at my desk. I ate lunch at my desk and I brought in food to nibble on while at my desk.

The second phase of the so-called Coaching Session was scheduled. They switched my principal accountabilities. I was told that I would keep my title and my pay but the work would be done by the white female assistant with no degree and my position required a bachelor's degree and three years' experience. I filed another EEO Complaint concerning this decision. Peg called me down and asked me not to say that the senior director approved this decision of switching my principal accountabilities. I stated to her that I distinctly asked you in in front of the director did the senior director approve this directive and you stated yes. I further asked you did he read the sheet you handed me with the revised principal accountabilities written on it and you said yes. I reminded Peg that I did not think this was ethical or legal and that is when she emphasized that the senior director was aware of this decision. As senior director he can change position tasks in his division. Peg also informed me that Lily had a nervous breakdown when they told her she would be doing my job. The select few did not expect that from Lily. The select few thought she would welcome the opportunity. According to Peg, Lily believe she could not do my job and they she would be overwhelmed. Peg stated she had to stay with Lily for over an hour to calm her down. This is not the first time Lily reacted hysterically to a situation. When questioned about my desk being broken into the director in his email to the senior director stated, "Lily was very upset that she was questioned by the police". During deposition the question arose, you sent Angelica to EAP because the police could not solve the case of her desk being broken into, but yet, Lilly have two outbursts which involves crying and screaming and yet no recommendation of sending her to EAP. The response from the director was he understood her being upset in both incidences and believes the need was not necessary. Again, evidence not submitted to the jury in court.

    As I reflect, I know it was only the grace of the Holy Spirit that carried me. Working a full-time job, doing my normal task and now the additional work of a secretary, carrying a full-time student load of three classes and maintaining a 3.8 average or higher, and going through the ministerial ordination process in my denomination. Somehow, I made it through; I filed two more EEO complaints in the midst of the ordeal. One for them training a white male summer intern and not giving me the same information in which I was a fulltime employee with almost fifteen years at the time. The other complaint was for the unfair work practices, unrealistic goals and other racist acts.

I was reprimanded because Human Resources had a CWEP program which they had females mostly minorities to assist you with typing, filing and data entry. Because I took the initiative and had one work with me, my white male supervisor was livid. He immediately called Human Resources and asked that they not send anyone to assist me. While he was explained to by Naomi from Human Resources that this is the purpose of the program, he wanted no parts of it and forbidden me from having any assistance. On that day, the young African American women who assisted me managed to file a box of files, update the data in the computer and typed labels. I messed their plan up for that week as it allowed me to catch up on my work. I wrote a memorandum asking to use the assistance from the CWEP program and I was never given a written response as to why I could not have assistance. When I wrote my next EEO complaint I included this incident and of course there was no response. Please note this is one of many items in the complaint that was not addressed.

The Performance Evaluation 2011

This action caused a major hiccup in the plan to terminate me as an employee, so phase three was implemented which as The Performance Evaluation. Instead of following corporate guidelines and adhering to the policy and practices they did everything but adhere to policy. First, my performance evaluation which is scheduled in June 16 was moved to March. I was called into the conference room given the performance evaluation and told to sign. I refused and took the performance evaluation home. My mistake was that I did not make copies of it as it was one of the most racist documents that I ever saw. The focus in the performance evaluation was on how I looked at my supervisor with a 'sullen look' and how his emphasis on that I did not fit in with the team. The team was he as my supervisor a white middle age male and the white middle age female assistant. Unfortunately, my home was broken into and only the documents were stolen at that particular break in.

Bear in mind that for years on my performance evaluation I always received the highest or near highest level for performance. I always had clear goals and exceeded them. I filed an employee complaint which is the process for the Performance Evaluation. I filed a memorandum in July 18, 2011 for a written response from Human Resources pertaining to the racist Performance Appraisal given by the supervisor and his neglect to adhere to corporate policy pertaining to my Performance Appraisal. I listed seven offenses in my memo dated July 18, 2011 and as of October 13, 2011 I still did not hear a response back from Human Resources.

I listed all the rules that were broken in the policy. Starting with no real goals set except that was given in the so-called Coaching Session which was stopped because of the EEO complaint filed. I absorbed the additional administrative task into my workload.

The May 2011 EEO & Human Resources Meetings

Because I filed another EEO complaint the EEO Manager and Human Resources wanted to meet with me thus, begun the three meetings of the May 2011 EEO and Human Resources sessions. They wanted to state that it was a personality difference not racial discrimination between the supervisor and me and me and the secretary. However, several of the so-called Coaching Sessions proved otherwise. There was the following of me to the restroom, but he did not follow the white secretary to the restroom. He trained a white male summer intern on a new form and process, did not train me, and openly admitted in front of human resources that he did train me and then turned around in the same meeting and stated I was responsible for knowing. He also compared my work to the white male summer intern that he took the time to train. I brought in the documents to show them the work and the comments that he made on the documents. On the third meeting, I brought in more evidence to share of the plot of how I was being treated and my work product. However, the meeting was moved to late afternoon. I brought a file cabinet with a lock and I placed the documents in there and went to lunch upon my return the lock on the file cabinet that I purchased was sawed through and the documents stolen. I filed a police report and had the police officer come over and look at the lock. Of course, I received no police report and this evidence was not submitted into court. However, this incident again made their plan to fire me very difficult.

Employee Assistance Program (EAP) The Grab & Go

Upon returning from vacation on March 23, 2012, I was met in my cubicle by the senior director who initially stated he was in my cubicle to ask a question pertaining to work. After the question was asked and answered I was asked by him to walk with him to Human Resources. I was startled because I had just returned from vacation and to my knowledge no incident had occurred. The senior director while I was sitting in my chair took me by my right arm which made me had to stand up and escorted me to the Human Resources conference room. Upon arriving at human resources, I was told I had to go to medical because of stress. I was shocked and surprised because I just returned from vacation and I was fine. The senior director was smiling while human resources was telling me this. I was shocked that this was happening for no apparent reason. The human resource person I will call her Peg asked the senior director to leave. His words to me are this is for my own good. When in essence he meant this was for his own good.

On March 23, 2012, Peg gave me a corporate policy which was written for front line personnel stating that their supervisor could send them to medical. There was no reason for them sending me to medical. Peg who is an African American female real job in human resources is to do the dirty work. Everyone knows when Peg shows up that it is trouble and that they send her to speak on their behalf. Peg told me to look at it this way that I will be home for as long as a year with pay and all I had to do is go see their doctor once a week. After a year, they would find me a job comparable to what I do and I would keep my pay. Peg told me to take advantage of the time off.

Well thank you Peg, but no thanks! Peg informed me that if I did not leave she would have security escort me out of the building. I must admit I was upset. When I woke up that morning my intention was not to be sent home and definitely not to be sent to medical. They finally got me! Or so they thought. Being sent to medical was used as a tool of oppression.

I called my daughter for her to pick me up. Upon her arrival, I broke down and cried in the car and at home. I am human and I was a victim of a sneak attack. I was a sweet innocent lamb for the slaughter. With no justification, they had set up an appointment for me in medical. My story stayed the same with every person that I saw. *"Today is the day that the senior director was supposed to give me a written response to my Performance Evaluation."* Instead I get sent to Medical and no one thinks that is strange. I was on vacation returned to work on Monday, no problem. Tuesday, I am sent to human resources then to medical. I saw the medical doctor and he stated I was fine. I shared the same story I was sent here because today is the day that the senior director was supposed to respond to my complaint in writing. The medical doctor stated he wanted no part of this and I was cleared by him.

I then had to see an EAP counselor; she had one goal in mind. She had her marching orders. I need to see their psychiatrist and have a full psychological evaluation. Please note, she did not speak with me nor did she want to hear why I was there she had her assignment you need to see our psychiatrist. I refused. I stated I will find my own doctor. Unfortunately, it takes time to look for a doctor and to get in on their calendar. Meanwhile, I was harassed every week until I saw the doctor it took almost two months. At one point they wanted to stop my pay if I did not see their doctor. In one of my weekly visits to see Helen the EAP counselor, I saw another African American female coworker that was seeing their doctor. They had her on medication and she was not herself. I was really shaken by what they had done to her. She was normally an outgoing, upbeat and energetic person. That day she seemed like she was sedated, tired and weak. I then realize this is what they wanted to do to me. God only knows what drugs they were giving her. There should be a way to get the list of drugs prescribed to African American females sent to EAP without giving their names.

On these weekly visits, it would be the same thing. My story never changed. "I was sent here because it was the day that I should have received a written response from the senior director pertaining to my performance evaluation". The counselor Helen was pretty much tired of me because they were pressuring her to have me see their doctor. I showed her proof that I had an appointment but I had to wait because I was not an emergency.

Helen decided I was not worth her time and she resorted to having me call her once a week. Meanwhile, I kept writing the company and asking questions pertaining to the policy that was handed to me. The more I read the policy the more I had questions. These questions were never answered and they were stolen from me. By stolen I mean documents taken from my home and documents deleted from my computer.

Furthermore, I still had more questions from reviewing the corporate policy on the performance evaluation as according to their own policy my employee rights were violated. I had a list of questions from the Performance Evaluation that were never answered and they were also stolen from me.

Likewise, being home I had the time to review the corporate policy for the Coaching Session and had further questions from that experience.

I finally received a response as to why I had not received the written response from the senior director pertaining to my performance evaluation. The response was that I would not receive a response until I return to work. Wow! I am so surprise. I did not receive a response because he did not have one.

Well, the day of reckoning was drawing near and their worst nightmare is about to happen. I was returning to work. So now they decided to let's play the stall game. They did not want to accept the letter from a Board Certified Psychiatrist that I was in good stable condition. They wanted to speak with her and they wanted me to sign that they could review my medical records. Again, I refused to sign. After speaking with my doctor who is a very nice professional and reminded me she has my best interest at heart and ethics would not allow her to speak to them in depth without a court order. I agreed to a narrow scope conversation and wrote on the form my intent. Please note on the form it states do not sign if you believe you are under duress. However, the threat was sign or you could not return to work. Please explain what does duress mean? With my forced permission and the threat lingering over my head, I signed and my doctor sent the bare essential information in writing. They then challenged my doctor the second time with her letter and she fought for me. I informed my attorney that my doctor was also an African American female and part of the challenge of accepting her diagnosis was because of color.

I was back with a smile. It took some doing but I had won that battle. This victory was not only for me, but also for the other African American females that they had sent to EAP who they had medicated and prevented them from being promoted.

The Father Document of May 2012

Conversely, a nice piece to the puzzle fell into my lap. For the purpose of this book, let's call it the Father Document. In my research to stay well-informed of things, I ran across it in the shared drive. I should have hit print and then read the document, but instead I read and then hit print. Would you believe in the middle of me reading they shut my computer shut off! The document did not print. I could not finish reading. But I know what I saw. It was The Father Document of May 2012. The reason they needed me out of my job was to move this document through without incident. I was an administrator and I would have or at least should have been a part of the administrative process.

The day I was scheduled to return to work was the day Father Document of May 2012 was presented to the Board of Directors and approved. No wonder they fought so hard to keep me out from work. I returned the week after the Father Document of 2012 was approved Board approved.

The Police Reports Filed and No Investigations

Although this conspiracy was conceived in 2011, it takes time to put everything in place especially when you have a fighter every step of the way. I survived the so-called Coaching Session of 2010, the March 2011 Performance Evaluation bashing, the May 2011 Human Resources and EEO personality conflict alternative to the structural racism and the 2012 EAP Medical Psychological scam. Also let me share I was experiencing continuous break-ins in my home and documents constantly being taken. The police reports are on file in my town from 2010 until present of the break-ins and other suspicious acts.

There is a side story of who I am and what I am about as an individual. I am the first one in my family to go to college and complete and not just stop with one degree but I have five. I saw obtaining a higher education as an investment in my future and laying a foundation for a standard for my children. I am a single divorced mother who started out as a temporary secretary and went to night school to better myself, provide for my family and be a good example for my children. On this meager pay, I was able to purchase my home and vehicle. While this is not a great accomplishment to some this is major considering I am the second oldest of six children. I was born in Baltimore, raised in Newark and graduated from East Orange High School. I am used to working hard for everything that I obtain. I do not mind putting in my time or starting from the bottom. I love my country and I come from a long line of family members who have served. I myself served as a civilian employee while my former husband served his country. My son and daughter in law recently were both honorably discharged from the service and are productive citizens contributing to society working and attending schools of higher education. I answered the call to ministry and made a conscious decision to serve the Lord. I know my reward is in heaven. I believe in sharing knowledge to invest in people and helping everyone in any way I can.

Prior to the selected few with their vicious attacks, I was able to enroll in the Employee Tuition Assistance Program for full-time employees, which paid for my both Bachelor's and Master's degrees in Public Administration. I graduated with Cum Laude with my Bachelor's and a 3.8 in the Master's Program. This served the company well as most of projects, reports and papers for school were work related. Prior to the new regime of 2008, most of my ideas were even implemented at work. I will share that I have had the opportunity to work with some knowledgeable people of different colors, religions, and ethnic groups' both male and female which contributed mutually to my educational and my professional growth.

Despite the opposition, I managed to endure from 2008 until 2012. The original plan was to take me out in 2012. But the

Storm of 2012 called Sandy happened! This impacted 24 states. The strategically placed police officers were ready for phase four but were diverted due to the storm. This impacted their work hours. After all, it was Captain Linden Weeks a company police officer that made the recommendation since he decided not to conduct an investigation of the wrongdoings in my cubicle to send me to Employee Assistance Program (EAP). I want to emphasize that I am stating that it was six company police officers involved. In the meantime, my home was being constantly broken into, documents taken and I was filing police reports.

This is when I noticed the numerous coincidences of the work emails and work telephone call requests parallels with my life. Every time I had a major event or appointment, I would receive a film, photo or event request for the exact same date. I also noticed the names and locations would be closed. This still occurs now. For example, while I am writing the book, I have received a request for February 10 which is the date of my National Women's organization event and my scheduled meeting in Philadelphia with my denomination. The request is from Black Dot. A previous example would be the film request in 2012 for EA Productions. The senior director has a twisted sense of humor. I will share more about him in a later chapter.

Other torture tactics were the height of my cubicle raised so that I am unable to see the exit sign in case of emergency, bed bugs in the light socket, blocking the work desk phone so that I would not receive any outside calls. The only outside calls were their crank calls that The Company police officers made. White powder at my desk and there was no investigation. I was originally told by Deemon Monstah the senior director that it was pollen and Deemon ordered my plants to be taken away from me. The senior director wanted them destroyed but maintenance did not want to be a part of that and they gave my plants to a coworker. Prior to that incident I had those plants for years and never had a problem. This was part of the biological warfare campaign.

The police and the other coconspirators now have to escalate to the next sphere which is my family and friends. They now needed the enlistment of strategically placed police officers to listen to conversations. Let me make a statement here. I appreciate and respect Police Officers they have a dangerous job and they protect the people. However, we must admit there are a few officers that make it bad for everyone else. It only takes one. In this case, it was six police officers strategically place to implement this diabolical plan. The last records I had were there were over 235 company police officers and I would not dare lump them all together. I have been crystal clear from the beginning and stated there were six police officers that illegally used their positions in the conspiracy against African Americans. I will speak more of the six company police officers in the next chapter.

But circling back to the discrediting the witness, I have a question. What does one do when the evidence is overwhelming and the witness is stable? You start noting in personal emails and memorandums about her stableness. Yes, you broke into her desk and stole items. Yes, you placed a tracker on her cell phone. Yes, you unscrewed her chair and loosed the credenza and how dare she reports those incidents to EEO and the police and have you questioned as a suspect. Well, I will fix her. I will have The Company police state they did not find any evidence to foul play and further make the recommendation for her to be psychologically evaluated. We need to have her removed because she is challenging the social order of the racist systems here. How dare she demand equal rights and equal protection of the law! Furthermore, how dare she demand that she be protected by the very ones that have been assigned to bring her down. Aah! The Company had the unsuspected victim and the perfect shield to hide behind. What better shield than a police shield to hide behind while we implement our racist acts. Just one stroke of the pen and she is gone out our hair forever. No pun on words, some of them are bald.

Oh no! she returned with a letter from a Board Certified Psychiatrist stating she is fine. Furthermore, the Board Certified Psychologist raised some questions which were never answered in court. Just because the police were inadequate in conducting their investigation why was she sent to a psychologist? Is that the normal policy? If Police have a case that they cannot solve the person who files the compliant is crazy. Let's pull all police records of unsolved cases and see how many of the complainants were sent for psychological evaluation.

No, I was sent to medical for two reasons. Reason one to get rid of me. Reason two because I was black and challenged the social order of the system. Back in October 2013, I was poisoned and needed to stay overnight in the hospital.

In November 2013, I was terrorized all night. They placed cats outside and while they howled all night it sounded like babies crying. The lights kept being turned on and off. There were sounds of people on the patio. Trash cans was being turned over. I was receiving constant mean crazy emails with threats. Days prior because they had my scheduled I would see several different funeral processions ride in front of me. They had a fleet of Ford Escalates that kept following me to make me feel intimidated. I was bombarded with junk mail that had death insurance policies and lawyers wanting to do my last will and testament. My cell phone was blocked. I received the email to withdraw the lawsuit. My bank accounts were blocked. My ATM cards did not work. I had been poisoned at work and had continuous break-ins my home. I had been poisoned so I had to throw all the food away at home. Family and friends received emails and texts that were mean and out of character and they thought they were from me. However, I did not send them. Family and friends were mad, hurt and upset with me.

This was a part of the isolation tactic. I was hungry, tired and stressed. I went to my attorney to ask to withdraw the case. He tried to talk me out of it. I signed the paper that I want to temporarily withdraw. I then went to work that day and the cruel vicious attacks still kept happening with the emails, the cell phone and biological warfare with the white powder at the desk I was isolated and placed in a conference room. They caged me like an animal. The senior director Deemon Monstah walked over with his fake grin and showed me a photo of Groucho Marx. I never liked that dry weak, demented sense of humor. While showing me the photo he told me governance, structure and having key players in place. I did not understand what he was saying at the time, but it makes sense now.

I thought it was over, once I signed to withdraw my case but in fact it was only the beginning of the evilness. I have been targeted as the experiment for the biological warfare and the economic injustice. I had withdrawn my case for nothing. I was the unsuspected.

Truth from the Grave

Can someone tell me why do you go to Police Internal Affairs? So that they can investigate police officers if a complaint was made. My brother medical benefits were cut off, his cell phone disconnected, and his money from social security was stopped. I stated this was done illegally by using Homeland Security. My brother passed away and the death was unknown. I asked for Internal Affairs to do an investigation. They did absolutely nothing. I gave them over 70 documents to review. To date, this matter still has not been addressed. This is called burying the evidence. Why was no investigation done? Why no written correspondence pertaining to the matter? Could it be I was correct in my inquiry that illegal tampering with the use

Homeland Security was done. Inquiring minds would like to know. This does not look good for the organization.

Their ignorance of the matter states that the matter is larger than what they can handle. One of the remedies in these kinds of matters is total ignorance. If we do not say anything or address it maybe it will go away. No, it shall not, it is like cancer it festers and grows deeper. Eventually, what is under the surface will rise to the top and be exposed. The hope is too much time has passed. No. The fact is you did nothing because you are guilty and it is never too late to right a wrong hence; this is why this book this is being written. So as it stands now, they have gotten away with murder. But this is only another African American male. So the evidence is buried without an investigation.

What you thought was buried has been resurrected. It is my hopes that we reveal the Truth from the grave and let the evidence speak for itself. The truth always rises and stands tall. Sometimes when you least expect it. Expect it. The other attacks on my family run the gamut from hitting the vehicles, towing our vehicles, changing appointments, tampering with our payments for utility bills, placing holds on deposits, having my granddaughter cell phone snatched out her hands, and having my older brother beaten and jaw broken. The latest is having my daughter and granddaughter surrounded by police, pushed against the fence, and then told they had the wrong person and in the computers to name a few.

While all of this was happening I was still putting in for other promotions and transfers and being denied. This information was brought up at disposition, but not mentioned at trial. I prepared a document that is in review at the senate subcommittee to address this issue. Normally when you have been placed on the "Black List" human resources with the consultation of the senior director devise a position for you. The title is changed. For example, if your complaint was about being a manager, human resources makes you a manager, but you are doing clerical work. It is work that is redundant and repetitious. The work has unrealistic deadlines and you are either given a supervisor with previous EEO complaints or known for being a taskmaster. In the secret unofficial meeting in which you are not invited the department is told that you are a trouble maker. Your coworkers out of fear stay away from you so they will not be labeled and have to endure the same punishment. This also ensures you have no support or assistance. The second phase of the heinous plan is isolation. This way they can say you do not work well with others and you are not a team player. The goal is to continuously write you up for not meeting standards and to prove you could not handle the position. The hopes is you retire or better yet for them you quit and lose benefits either way the institution wins and the ultimate goal met which is your removal.

      Some people may wonder why I stayed so long. Someone need to stand up for what is right. I too am entitled to retirement and benefits. I too do not want to lose my benefits after working for a company for over 20 years.

Chapter Two

Without A Shadow of Doubt

For his letters, say they, are weighty and powerful...
II Corinthians 10:10[ii]

The Letters I wrote to various entities throughout the state and Washington, D.C. are powerful and weighty. Little did I know at the time, that the Post Office I was using had been compromised and none of my letters was being sent to their designated locations. All of my letters were sent to one person the senior director, who decided which ones he would respond to if any. If I received a response it would direct me back to The Company. The letters I sent were certified receipt, some would be signed but with signatures you could not read. Therefore, over the years I invested money into the US Postal System and it was a waste. Towards the end of this terrible sage, one of the breakthroughs was in some instances if I could I would hand deliver the letters. In this town, as things continued to spiral I could take photos of incidents and hand deliver them to the mayor's office. Nonetheless, this issue was not resolved but they cannot deny that they were informed.

EEO Complaints

There were eight Equal Employment Opportunities complaints filed and not one issue in the complaints were addressed. Instead they used the tactic and combine them together within one letter when the complaints were specific and listed individually. It did not make a difference because the complaints and letter were not submitted in court. The jury never saw any documents nor given any evidence.

During deposition the question was asked of Demon Monster did he touch me or escort me down to Human Resources. He stated I was informed. This was not brought at trial that he <u>grabbed</u> my arm and escorted me to Human Resources. I filed my complaint on May 18, 2013.

Police Reports

I was terrorized all night until I withdrew lawsuit October 2013
03.22.17 The flood of all the unnecessary threats should just cease. The criminals have done everything under the sun to my family and me. The latest threat is breaking into my house again <u>(police reports)</u>, having someone hit me and using the University Medical Research Team chemical warfare causing me to become ill at work and needing an ambulance. Just check the Board Approved Father Document and The Company Police Homeland Security technical list and end this.

The Discovery

During discovery several pieces of information were brought to light however when it came time to share this pertinent information in court evidence was considered not admissible. As you read through this book you will see the list of evidence escalating.

The Lynching

In 2011, the white secretary Lily had a cartoon of snowman with a scarf around his neck as a noose and a park bench kicked over. Underneath the capture was written "I had enough!" Before I went on vacation I received an email from the white administrative assistant about my work performance, me not being a team player and that my analysis of question pertaining the falsifying the numbers of the amount work we received was "unacceptable" to her. I realize that the email came from the senior director who forwarded to the administrative assistant to pretend as if it came from her. The senior director does this quite frequently. He hides behind other people and tell them to do what he really would like to do.

This serves two purposes. One he believes that there will be no direct link to him should the person get caught or confronted and secondly because of his weak and cowardly personality he can express his self through another person as this is called manipulation and abuse of position and power. I would have ignored the email, but since she stated this was "unacceptable" to her she empowered herself to be my supervisor. Since she believes she had earned that right to write me her thoughts, I in turn should have the same equal rights. I need to remind the administrative assistant that she was removed from her previous position because she did not get along with the office manager who also was a white female. This is where that personality disagreement could have been used between to white females.

In my email to Lily I reminded her that according to her job description she was to assist me hence her title administrative assistant. I was an administrator and my position required a bachelor degree and three years' experience. I held at the time a Master's degree in Public Administration. Lily has no degree. Her function was to type labels, data entry and file. I explained to her my analysis that the supervisor and her had devised the policy for weekly numbers for the same request that could be done monthly. I informed her that the unethical practice in this department in falsifying numbers were "unacceptable" should The Company decide to do an audit on the work. Moreover, since she copied the supervisor, I too copied the supervisor. The supervisor informed me that Lily will be very upset when she returns from vacation and see my email. As she sent her email and went on vacation. I told the supervisor that I hope Lily learned her lesson and will think twice about writing me an email as if I am her subordinate. Notice he thought nothing about me being upset and receiving the email from Lily. He was concerned about her feelings and receiving an email from me stating her email to me was unacceptable. This brings us full circle to why the senior director had Lily display that racist cartoon. The senior director had enough!

At work they exploit your ideas, education and skills. There are major disparities, racial biases that infect their decision-making ability. There is no exercise of discretion decisions are unchecked.

Performance Appraisal

My Performance Appraisal was stolen from my mail from home, broke my lock on my mailbox. My desk at work was broken into and personal file cabinet that I purchased the lock was sawed and broken as well. I filed a police report and had The Company police officer come and see for himself. What happen to Officer Saul Drew who witnessed both desk drawers locks broken? Did he lie on the Police Report as well? Why wasn't this information allowed in court?

This information along with several other relevant information never made it to court. At my home the front door lock was broken and puzzle pieces were found around the house.

Letters Written

While I was diligent in seeking assistance in this national matter of domestic terrorism, I did not realize at the time that my letters were being illegally diverted at the United States Post Office and given to Deemon Monstah to respond. In most cases, I received no response to my letters. In a few cases, the response I received was to deal with The Company that was terrorizing me.

- On September 29, 2014 I wrote a letter to the Transportation Commissioner of The Company and the Board Office. *"...As I have discovered the following things that are far beyond the scope of this discrimination and harassment lawsuit. This case involves conspiracy, terrorism, and commingling of federal funds to name a few."*

- On October 13, 2015 I wrote the Governor Fetter and gave him the list of names of who was violating my constitutional rights, invading my privacy and stated that their illegal practices are a threat to National Security.

- On March 3, 2016 I wrote the former Governor Harvey Fetter, the Director of Homeland Security, and the Transportation Commissioner.

Governor Harvey Fetter
125 State Street
City, The State

- On April 19, 2016, I wrote the US Attorney General seeking assistance from that office.

US Attorney General
U.S. Department of Justice
950 Pennsylvania Avenue, NW
Washington, DC 20530-0001

- On May 4, 2016, I wrote The Company Board of Directors. Here is a quote from the letter. *"I am being terrorized by a select few here at The Company because of the technology used from the Board Approved Father Document."*

- On July 25, 2016 I wrote the following pertaining to the Homeland Security abuse and racial profiling of my daughter and me.

Governor's Office
Common Ground for Virginia
P.O. Box 1475
Richmond, VA 23218

Virginia Police Internal Affairs
Municipal Center, Building 11
2509 Princess Anne Road
Virginia, Beach VA 23456

Homeland Security Washington, DC
245 Murray Lane SW
Washington, DC 20223

Other Letters mailed:

Director, Office of Homeland Security of State
Transportation Commissioner of State

Federal Transit Administration
Office of Civil Rights
Attention: Complaint Team
East Building, 5th Floor – TC
1200 New Jersey Avenue, SE
Washington, DC 20590

U.S. Department of Justice
950 Pennsylvania Avenue, NW

Washington, DC 20530-0001

Court

One would hope for an impartial judge, I received a white racist female judge who tried the case before it got started. I was made fun of by the judge and ridiculed because of my religion. The trial was a joke and they made a mockery of the legal system.

After submitting years of evidence to support my case, it was all denied. So none of the evidence submitted seen the light of day in the court room. From my performance reviews dating back from 2003 to 2008 to my resume, neither my communication experience nor training was allowed to be submitted. No samples of my work products in communications were even mentioned. No job description submitted. I was limited to discussing three items, the lynching which was chalked up as no big deal and I was not allowed to express how I felt about seeing the lynching and share the history behind what lynching means to me as an African American.

Men would be snatched out of homes, beaten, hung and set on fire in front of their families and no one was allowed to say anything. The reasons for these atrocities could range from a white person saying you looked them in the face, you stole something for your family or you supposedly lied on a white person. Even if any of this is true, it is still no justification for genocide, enduring the humiliation of being snatched out of your home, hung and then placed on fire all under the guise of 'the law". I followed the law, I filed eight EEO complaints, and I sat through EEO meetings and Human Resources. I endured the photo of seeing a lynching and the ultimate blow in the court room where I had to see the senior director with the smile painted on his face as the judge continuously denied justice and excusing the jury. While I was not snatched out of bed, I was terrified out of my home. While I was not humiliated by being dragged into the street, I was humiliated to suffer through the psychological exam based on a racist police officer too incompetent to do his job and an investigation. While I was not set on fire, I was threatened to be fired numerous times and the intense elevation of these traumatic failed attempts. I was impacted by the racist photo. The sad shame is this happened in 2015 and not 1815. Just as the snowman was left hung, hanging in the balance lifeless and eyes rolled to back of his head, I too was left lifeless with no justice. I believe lady liberty with the blindfold had her eyes rolled to the back of her head. My head dropped as I was denied my opportunity to speak about my feelings, my heritage and what was done to me.

08.03.17 Back on 2013 When The Company broke into my house to steal documents such as my performance evaluations from 2003 -2008, Leo Smart's letter recommending me to Manager and Deemon Monstah letter stating the promotion of Nick Stelton and Ivon Nice. They jammed my front door and my key did not fit. Let's hope this is not another recurrence of the 2013 incident. Again, I ask the question what do you think I have in my home that you are trying to so desperately to break in and steal?

Today I am receiving a series of emails. The last time I received an email series the next day four helicopters hovered over my home. Again, I ask the question. What do you believe I have in my home that requires land surveying and photos?

The performance evaluation where the judge stated just because I did not agree with the racist remarks if my supervisor told me to sign the performance evaluation I should have signed it and the other issue discussed was my supervisor training a white male summer intern and not training me. The judge stated in the end I received the information that I needed whether it came from the then supervisor or the summer intern did not matter.

The Draft

In the document I wrote for the Resolution for African Americans Development & Career Advancement Recommendation for Executive Order to be signed by the new Governor and to revise the company Corporate Policies which was forwarded to a senate subcommittee for economic justice on page 3, I referenced this thought. *"The public and psychological damage done to African Americans and other Black Americans because of select privilege given to a select few emerged into this new caste system that has caused an economic injustice."*

I further state that *"In light of our nation's racial history, the question is not do this exists, but how can we dismantle it here. As this company in the United States history will judge this corporation harshly if it does not engage its energies in the battle for racial progress. If we ever hope to abolish the racism in this company, we must recognize and address the issues stated."*

I never had a chance to submit the evidence to the jury. I did receive a fair trial. The whole thing was a game to Deemon. Everyone was on the Governor's payroll and just went through the motion. The outcome was already decided before the court date was set. They waited until the day before to decide that all my crucial evidence was inadmissible. Reason being there was no interest in hearing the truth. They knew without a shadow of a doubt that if I had a fair trial and could submit all the evidence I would have won my case. The whole week was spent on recess, excusing the jury and insulting my religion and any statement that I made. To my surprise it was mostly done by the judge who is good friends with you guessed it Deemon Monstah and both report to the Governor.

Chapter Three

The Unveiling

Give a man a mask and he'll tell you the truth. Oscar Wilde

What do you do when the ones that are supposed to protect you are the ones committing the crimes? If they are placed strategically throughout the state, what do you do? While we are worried about foreign terrorists from other countries, we have domestic terrorism right here in the work place. Who polices the police? My life is more in danger with the select few than from any outside terrorist. The domestic terrorists are far worst because they have access. They monitor your phone, your computer and track your vehicle.

The four entities partnered together the university with the medical research, the University of Engineering, the advertising company and the A & Z Transportation Company. This is the part of the book that most people flip through because they believe it is too technical. However, if you want to understand the capability you should read this section thoroughly and slowly. In fact, take notes and ask questions. This is basically Biology 101 and Psychology 101, which lays the groundwork for understanding technology and how it is used to tap into human beings. Biopsychology is the branch of psychology concerned with discovering the biological process that give rise to our thoughts, feelings and actions. Below are some questions based on general known information to ask to raise awareness about the medical ethics, human rights and the constitutional rights of individuals and the capability that is given to people without checks and balances.

What is the connection between our Central Nervous System and Communication Cell Towers?

Science has now found a way to mimic the human cell structure with cell towers. From your brain and down your spinal cord is the Central Nervous System (CNS). Signals can travel along the spinal cord acts between the brain and the rest of the body. The spinal cord is the fiber cable or conduit. This can be done in split seconds. With everything being computerized this technology can be used in humans, cars, and bridges to name a few. One would have to wonder with this technology how would this impact the Crossover Tunnel scandal?

How do you process the conversion from a cell tower to a human cell?

Both human and computers give off electrical signals. Human signals are interpreted by our Central Nervous System. We have nerve cells that communicate with each other. A computer can tap in, receive, and interrupt that signal in both humans and computers.

Can Communication cabling systems control our human bodies? Yes, both communication cable and the spinal column are affected by the frequency of action potentials (electrical event in a cell). One performs in a telecommunication cabinet the other in a human nerve cell. Peripheral Nervous System (PNS) communication lines called nerves carry signals into and out of the Central Nervous System (CNS) which is now interchangeable with computer technology.

What does the Cognition of humans have to do with technology? Cognition is the ability of the nervous system to perceive, store, process, and use information gathered by sensory receptors. Their influence is indirectly through chemical reactions in the brain moving via the spinal cord. Hormones affect target cells by two main signaling mechanisms which are the Endocrine System through the blood or the nervous system through the spinal cord.

In addition, science technology has discovered a way to chemically breakdown down molecules and move inanimate objects such as paper, pens, money and identification cards. They have not discovered a way to chemically breakdown the human body so these types of items have to have skin contact so they cannot remove them. As you read this book you will read of incidents that these type of occurrences happened. People wonder why I carry my keys, identification and money in my hand or place them on my body for skin contact to keep them from physically taking these items away from me. Ask the company do they have this capability and have they been allowing a select few to misuse this technology.

THE KEY

What does the Nervous System transmit? The Nervous System transmits electrical signals via nerve cells. When a nerve signal reaches the end of a nerve cell, it triggers the secretion of molecules called neurotransmitters. The synapse or the junction, or relay point between two neurons or between a neuron and effector cell is the key to the Nervous System. These same electrical signals can be transmitted through technology.

Why is the Nervous System compared to a tiny circuit board? The membrane of a neuron resembles a tiny circuit board, receiving and processing multiple bits of information in the form of neurotransmitter molecules. This living circuit board account for the nervous system's ability to process data and to formulate appropriate responses to stimuli. Some of the stimuli are light, heat, and cold.

How is physical energy converted into signals our Nervous System can understand? Physical energy is converted in signals which our nervous system can understand through highly specialized cells known as sensory receptors located in our eyes, ears, nose, tongue and skin which are responsible for accomplishing this coding task. Light, heat, sound, smell is some of the physical energy.

THE DOOR

What passes through cells at Electrical Synapses? Action potential passes between cells at electrical synapses. Electrical synapses move at lightning speed. Electrical synapses, action potential themselves pass from one neuron to the next. The receiving neuron is stimulated quickly and always at the same level (frequency) of the action potential as the sending neuron. Examples are the heart and digestion. Chemical Synapses are prevalent in most other organs, where signaling among neurons is complex and varied. Neurons can carry pain signals and caused what is called **referred pain**.

What makes up the peripheral nervous system? The Cranial and Spinal Nerves make up the peripheral nervous system.

What is the signal? The signal is the wavelike change in membrane potential, the self-perpetuated action potential that regenerates sequentially at points farther and farther away from the site of stimulation. Action potential ions move across the neuron membrane in a direction perpendicular to the direction of the impulse along the neuron.

THE WELCOME MAT

Biopsychology is the branch of psychology concerned with discovery of the biological processes that give rise to our thoughts, feelings, and actions. Medical Science and technology can now via the spinal cord tap into this process.

Where is the spinal cord located? What does it do? The spinal cord, which lies inside the vertebral column, or spine, receives sensory information from the skin and muscles and integrates simple responses to certain kinds of stimuli.

How does a synapse ensure that signals pass only in one direction from a sending neuron to a receiving cell? The signal can go only one way at any one synapse because only the sending neuron releases neurotransmitter, and only the receiving cell has receptors for the neurotransmitters.

What is a hormone? Chemical signals to regulate body activities in Endocrine cells. A hormone is a regulatory chemical that travels in the blood from its production site and affects other sites in the body, often at the same distance. Hormones are made and secreted mainly by organs called endocrine glands.

What is an Endocrine cell? The endocrine cells are full of molecules of the hormone. The endocrine cell secretes the molecules directly into the circulating system. The molecules travel in the blood to the target cells, cells that respond to this hormone.

What can a single hormone molecule do to a target cell? A cell single hormone molecule can dramatically alter a target cells metabolism by turning on the production of a number of enzymes. A tiny-amount of a hormone can govern the activities of enormous numbers of target cells in a variety of organs. In other words, you can alter a person's thoughts or behavior via technology if you target certain cells.

What are the two types of regulating systems? And why is Timing Important? Hormones and Neurotransmitters are the two types of regulatory systems. The Endocrine System may take minutes, hours, or days to act. Neurotransmitters do not travel in the blood stream they move across the synapse where they bind to receptor sites. **The nervous system provides split-second control.**

THIS IS THE DANGER THAT TECHNOLOGY HAS OVER HUMAN BEINGS.

What is a local regulator? A local regulator is a neurotransmitter chemical signal. If secreted into the body fluid and affects cells very near the point of secretion. Local regulators called ***prostaglandins*** are made by nearly all cells and have a variety of function. Prostaglandins secreted by the placenta cause the nearby muscles of the uterus to contract, helping induce labor during child birth.

What should we know about neurosecretory cells? A second type of hormone-secreting cell is the neurosecretory cell is a specialized nerve cell that in addition to conducting nerve signals makes and secretes hormones. Like endocrine cells, **neurosecretory cells release hormones into the blood for transport to target cells.**

What makes up the Endocrine System? And why is this important? Collectively, all hormone-secreting cells constitute the Endocrine System the body's main chemical-regulating system because hormones are carried in the blood. **This is important because they reach all parts of the body. The Endocrine System controls whole-body activities by secreting into the blood.**

Why are Action Potentials "All-or-none events"? Action potentials are "all or none events" because they are the same no matter how strong or weak the stimulus (light, heat, sound, and other types of physical energy) that triggers them. There are three states of potential in a cell which is: The **Resting Potential** the voltage across the plasma membrane of a resting neuron. This is normally about -70 millivolts. The **Action Potential** is the technical name for a nerve signal and electrical changes in a cell. The **Threshold Potential** which is normally at -50 millivolts. The difference between the **threshold potential** and the **resting potential** is the minimum change in the membranes voltage that is needed most to generate the **action potential.**

The spinal cord can be compared to a communication site. Hence the name cell tower. The protected inside of the bony vertebrae of the spine is an inch-thick gelatinous bundle of nerves fibers. This structure, called the spinal cord acts as the central communication conduit between the brain and the rest of the body. Millions of nerve fibers carry motor information from the brain to the muscles, while other fibers bring sensory information (such as touch, pain, and body position) from the body back to the brain.

Cabling is important! It is the frequency of action potentials that changes with the intensity of stimuli. Once your central nervous system receives information in the form of action potentials, it can process the information to formulate a response to it. The Central Nervous System (CNS) depends on the sensory neurons passing their signals to other neurons in the CNS. The Nervous System is just another cable transferring information.

Chemical Warfare involves using the toxic properties of chemical substances as weapons.

Neuroscience is neurochemistry experimental psychology, which deals with the structure of the nervous system and brain.

Neurochemistry is the study of neurochemical including neurotransmitter and other molecules such as psychopharmaceuticals and neuropeptides that influence the function of neuron.

Biological Warfare or Germ Warfare is biological toxins or infectious agents such as bacteria, viruses, and fungi with the intent to kill or incapacitate.

Are illegal cognitive experiments being performed without consent or knowledge of individuals? If so, this is an unethical violation, constitutionally illegal and an invasion of privacy.

The Human Sacrificed for Science Experiment

Do you think science that involves human beings and technology has gone too far? Should we be concern with the ethics? What is the government's responsibility concerning having access to thoughts?

How did this unfold, and I how did I figure this all out? As previously mentioned, I do hold five degrees. Also, I mentioned this is basic Biology 101 and Psychology 101. Moreover, I have been in this position involving communications since 2003. I was also given training to work on the communication aspect of my position. Compiled with me being an employee for over twenty years, I was able to sit down and put the pieces of the puzzle together. One line holds true in business. Follow the money, when you follow the money look at peoples' account of who made a withdrawal and who made a deposit within the same week or month the picture becomes clear. In addition, when you investigate dummy companies and look at the signatures of who signs it all becomes crystal clear.

The Senior Director Deemon Monstah was the driving force of this conspiracy from conceptualization to implementation to its near completion. In this diabolical plan, they had no exist plan as their plan was to torture me via technology for the rest of my life. How dare I challenge the so-called elite! This is why it is imperative that the Federal government step in because if this happens to me I am sure there are others in similar situations.

I know that I am being monitored while writing this book so the distorted culprit is distraught and you can best believe he is plotting another deceptive plan that involves disrespecting me as a female, undermining my story and further destructive action against my finances all via illegal use of Homeland Security technology.

I want to pause here to speak concerning Homeland Security. I am not challenging the government in their decisions and the interactions of Homeland Security since I admit this is out of my realm of experience and knowledge. I want to be clear I am speaking to the abuse and misuse that has occurred concerning Homeland Security technology as it has fallen into racist hands here in the United States. This technology in the wrong hands has given a select few unlimited power to manipulate the system that was designed to protect us as United States citizens. I also what to state I am not against Homeland Security technology. I am against the select few that have used it illegally. I am against the select few that have been entrusted to serve and protect, but instead threaten, lie and steal. I am against the misuse of system that has not given a person a way of escape in a situation like this. Where do you go when someone misuse their position and power? I went to several state entities and to no avail I was sent back to The Company that is assaulting me. There has to be a way to correct this system. There has to reform and attention given to this urgent matter. I know I am not the only one suffering while I may be the only one speaking up and speaking out about it.

My question to Washington, DC what are you going to do about this situation? We cannot allow a few demented racist to have access to technology and power that they cannot handle. As child, if you could not handle what was given to you, it was taken away. I am asking as a start that you take away the power, disconnect his resources and conduct a thorough investigation into matter with someone who is not associated with the state. As I have undertaken previous assaults and survived, I will defeat him in his next fiendish scheme.

When you read my story note they did not stop with adults. They attacked the elderly, the disable, young children and babies. They went after anyone that was an African American and were connected to me. I just want to be free from evil and from their sin. Because I was being attacked daily from every possible angle by a gang of domestic terrorists I have organized the abuse within several different categories. You will see a great deal of overlapping as the vicious attack was designed to take not only family but my friends and me out as well. I included the dates so there can be a chronological order. With the gang of twelve being strategically placed, you will see that on many of the days more than one thing occurred, so you will see the same date in different categories. You may need to review the beginning of this chapter again in order to digest some of the incidents you may read concerning the technology. While I want to state again, my issue is not with Homeland Security. My grave concern is for the people entrusted to use Homeland Security technology and there not be any regulations, oversight and supervision for when a person misuse or abuse their trust illegally and cause harm to the people they are supposed to protect. I am more than a human sacrifice for a science experiment or an object that is toyed with because I am an African American female. There is no justification of what have been done to my family and me. None! I am someone's mother, grandmother, sister. I am a human being! My human life has value and my privacy should not be snatched from me because someone else's issues, weaknesses and insecurities for being confronted for his racial wrongs.

Technology Abuse

07.25.16 My home and work emails, personal and work cell phone are still being tampered with along with emails and texts being deleted and altered.

10.18.16 I just received a voicemail message using my social security number as the return call. These are the type of threats I receive prior to some illegal activity being done such as Identity Theft with my social security number.

10.19.16 Via the illegal use of technology, I was informed that I will not have use of my cell phone, laptop or any technology. I am encouraging everyone I speak to write their congress person pertaining to the illegal use of federal funds for personal racial vendettas and depriving me of my constitutional rights. How many African Americans have this illegal use of Homeland Security technology been used against? Washington needs to investigate this State starting with the company police. My question is why would you give local company police officers this type of federal equipment?

10.21.16 The misappropriation of the company resources, Federal Funds and Homeland Security technology continues: During a real terroristic threat they can shut down technology such as my laptop and cell phone. They can also shut down utilities such as water, electricity and sewer. In my case, they are doing the opposite having the water run, pipes clogged, and lights come on.

This is all done to increase my utility bills and cause a financial hardship. Deemon Monstah has made it up in his mind I should not have anything, so he seeks to find means and ways to steal my money and The Company allows it. The economic injustice runs from high utility bills to repairs caused by them in the home or vehicles. Such as my daughter's tire ripping apart causing her to be late for her job interview. On the next day, the other tire ripped apart to cause my daughter not to pick up her Driving Certificate and her daughter from school. The cost is another $30 for another used tire until she is able to afford a better tire. The personal vendetta against my daughter is because she is my family.

The Advertising Company intersected my parent's moving truck and stole items off of the moving truck. The actual move was November 2014 and I started writing letters on January 7, 2015 after the items were delivered. This is another federal offense in which it was approved by the former Governor Harvey Fetter as the furniture was supposed to be delivered from Maryland. In trying to file a claim, my mail was intersected from the US Post Office, and it was Deemon Monstah that responded to all my letters. My father had insurance for full reimbursement for lost items. My father paid the additional insurance to ensure his items were covered and Deemon Monstah stole the items and the insurance money with the help of company Police and the advertising company. He robbed the elderly because they were my parents.

Here are some other economic injustices that were done to cause me a hardship.
My Roth account was tampered with again. A fee of $105 was charged and when the bank tried to remove it, they were placed on hold for over 30 minutes. In addition, the $25 a month transfer to this account was also stopped. My credit report was stolen as I will find on it identity theft as Deemon was allowed to ruin my credit with fake charges, late fees, and place a lien on my property via technology. Because of the relationship with the former Governor Harvey Fetter, Deemon Monstah with the assistance of Holden Mitch Chief Information Officer of Technology and certain company police officers is allowed to continually abuse the system. Holden Mitch has a security clearance and uses it at will to violate my constitutional rights and invasion of privacy. Holden should be held accountable and responsible for all acts that they allow Deemon Monstah to commit using his security clearance. The question today for the company is how long and how deep in will it allow Deemon Monstah to drag it down. It is known that Deemon Monstah is bipolar and suffer from depression along with other psychological issues (review his past and personally life) and The Company continues to allow him to hold a position and make poor and dangerous decisions on behalf of The Company.

The ultimate goal in this was for me to quit and to be broke. I refuse to do either.

11.09.16 Homeland Security Technology – Illegal wiretap into my personal calendar: Also, I noted the consistent changes in my work requestor's date requests for events coincide with dates in my personal calendar. When an analysis is done of my personal calendar and that of my work request calendar you will see the correlation. Please note while you need just cause, a judge and warrant the select few has bypass all of the legal proceedings to violate my human rights.

11.09.16 My Women's Organization information has been deleted from my computer and personal email.

Traffic Abuse

Because of the illegal access to my personal calendar, cell phone and emails they knew all my appointments. So on days where I had appointments, meetings, or a special event there would be construction, road blocks, cars stalled, roads closed, detours and police delaying traffic. I had learned to expect my own delays just like Crossover Tunnel traffic scandal.

Bus Abuse

Because of the illegal use of technology and tampering with the bus schedules and traffic, this places passengers and the public at risk and in danger.

12.17.15 The 5pm Express Bus was detoured by city police per the company police request from Deemon Monstah on 12.16.15 to use an alternative route and wait in traffic. The Bus could have stayed on course and avoided protestors. The delay was 1hr and 30 minutes. I had an important church meeting to attend on this day and I missed it.

12.18.15 At the expense of the company, taxpayers and Bus commuters the 4:15pm & 4:29pm was a no show at the Station.

12.30.15 The bus tried to leave me at 4:15pm. Question: Why is there a detour on a major street during rush hour? Why weren't customers notified in advanced. The detour took the bus into more traffic to delay service.

01.05.16 I boarded the Bus at 7:50 am and was on time to arrive at 7:52 am. However, I did not arrive to until 8:40 am. This ride took 50 minutes and it is normally a 30 minute or less ride.

03.10.16 Delays in traffic the same tactic used on the state level. The federal internal investigation will show a correlation between my travels to meetings/functions and the dates of traffic jams.

03.15.16 The normal bus I take was intentionally delayed today.

03.21.16 I have another meeting today, so my bus is late again.

04.22.16 Bus scheduled for 4:30pm and 4:45pm was both a no show. I saw two buses ride by, but the signs were different. It is believed that the buses changed their signs at the Penn Station stop.

07.29.16 The bus was a "no show" and did not arrive today at the scheduled time of 6:20 am. I took another bus at 6:30am. No reason was given for the no show bus. The purpose of sharing the bus abuse is to show the fact that this abuse not only impacts me, but anyone on the line who needs to take the bus.

08.19.16 In past experiences Deemon has been allowed to use his position and authority as senior director to impact bus service. This morning is no different. My bus did not show up and the alternate bus was late. In addition, due to mismanagement there was no call placed to control center to inform the bus driver on the 70 Bus that there was an accident and to be detoured. This type of behavior impacts service and jeopardize the image of The Company. In addition, this has racial implications as it looks like service for poor people and people of color does not matter especially in urban areas. Would this type of treatment occur if the bus was coming from the Southern portion of the state? Please take into consideration the consequences and repercussions of the poor business decisions being made to impact me as I use public transportation. On a bus run that holds 55 people seated and 20 standees can have over 100 people or more from the beginning to the end of the trip. Is the company willing to endanger the lives of over 100 people, their performance record, and the public image of the company because of one person's hatred of blacks?

12.16.16 Deemon is allowed to tamper with the bus schedule again. This also impacts on-time performance the buses.

Personal Abuse

One of the things that Deemon does is to take departmental photos. This is a facade to show that he is not a racist and to show diversity in the department. Please view the photos carefully. In the original photos there were thirteen people. Of the thirteen people eight were managers or above. All of the managers and above were white, had less experience and less time in the company. This was one of my EEO complaints. So recently the senior director promoted a person of color, but he has the lowest managerial position of his peers. Although he has the most years, the most experience, the most degrees and the best qualified to be at director level or above. So now out of fourteen people in the departmental photo we have one entry level manager. Because another one of my complaints was not promoting African American females, Deemon has hired two more African American females. Please check the pay scales of these females along with my pay scale and you will see that we all fall below comparable what our white colleagues who are similarly situated earns.

Back in October 2013, I was terrorized all night. They placed cats outside to sound like babies. My lights were being turned on and off in my home. The alarm on the door kept going off and the trashcan was being knocked over. I was consistently receiving emails. The days prior because they had my schedule they were have funeral processions at every location I attended. I was bombarded with death benefits from insurance company. Lawyers were sending me applications for my last will and testaments. My bank accounts were blocked. I could not get money from the ATMs nor could I use my debit card. I had been poisoned at work and spent the night in the hospital. Meanwhile the break-ins in my home continued. The food was also poisoned in my home and I had to throw it away. I filed numerous police reports in my town. My family and friends received emails and texts from me that I did not send so they were upset with me because of the messages I later found were very unpleasant and out of character for me. I was hungry, tired and had not money that I could access even though I was getting paid. I finally did like the emails requested and went to my attorney to withdraw the case. He tried to talk me out of it and suggested I go to the police. I shared it was the police who were terrorizing me. My attorney had me signed temporary withdrawal. I then went to work that day and the cruel vicious attacks still kept happening with the emails, the cell phone and the biological warfare. I thought it was over because I signed to stop the lawsuit, it was only the beginning of the evilness.

02.10.16   Deemon my stole bear claw gloves. These are gloves I wear in the extreme cold weather while waiting for the bus. I received a call from IRS stating I had responded to their letter. On numerous occasions mail has been stolen out of mail box. I believe the letter from IRS was stolen from my mailbox. While this will seem petty, Deemon despises African American males. He wants to keep them down and out at any cost. So out hatred for Black males Deemon steals grandson's homework. Homework is worth one fourth of a student's grade. If you can master the homework you can master the concept.

04.22.16 As I shared in the beginning of this chapter some of the technical advances one being the deterioration of an item. So, as I walked home because my bus was a no show the shoes I wore were targeted for deterioration.

09.19.16 As it is known that The Company police has the technology to black out telephones as part of Homeland Security for protection on transportation. The selected few is currently illegally using this technology and blacking out my personal cell phone. I have been to Verizon twice to have the telephone checked. It works temporarily while inside of Verizon. Once I leave the property it of course blacks out. The purpose of this is because the culprits are afraid that I will forward information to every one of the corrupt illegal abuse of technology and tax payers' money. I am not afraid of them anymore nor am I am afraid of telling the truth. The public should be made aware of what a selected few racists have the abusive power to do here in America. They are domestic terrorists and should be prosecuted to the fullest extent of the law. These are company police officers, a no passing the bar lawyer and representatives of The Company. I have been very direct from the beginning in the listing of who they are and have been. The select few which compiles as six police officers and five people strategically placed in the company and the former Governor Harvey Fetter.

09.26.16 All of my technology is still illegally blackout. This morning's interesting twist is my ID that was <u>stolen</u> miraculously showed up on my property today. When I got to work I inadvertently used it and it was taken by security. Coincidence, I think not. This is a conspiracy to give license to continue harassment. And speaking of license, why not produce the Board Approved Father Document from 2012.

09.21.16 My personal cell phone and laptop still illegally blackout by these terrorists. Today is the deadline to register for an organization trip to Washington DC to see the White House, African American Museum and MLK Memorial. Their fear is I would share their illegal use and abuse of Homeland Security with someone in Washington, D.C. Their fear is correct, if I had an opportunity to present this information I certainly would have.

11.15.16 As I unfortunately continued to endure the harassment and the abuse of illegal use of technology from the economic injustice and hardship. My electric bill has doubled as it is generated via technology and my water bill has quadrupled. As previously stated Deemon has decided to steal money from my family and me by any means. He strongly believes that the economic injustice is the only way to utterly destroy me.

12.21.16 Starting from last night the latest technology abuse is to have my personal cell phone continuously go off with alarm every time I say or do something or someone stated something that Deemon does not like. I attended a NAACP meeting and Kwanza Celebration. As the speakers were sharing information their cell phone would intentionally go off if something was said that the police did not like. Such as the university owned slaves and sold the parents of slaves to help build the university. The university was built on the backs of African Americans. The cell phone is a tracking device. It monitors my location and as longs it is on it can also pick up other signals. I like most people keep their cell phones with them. I am unable at this point to turn my cell off.

Work Abuse

01.11.16 The domestic terrorist games continue. While all of my white coworkers went to Texas, I complained of the unfair practice. The senior director came up with the deceptive idea of a phony trip to Texas. So that it would appear that the senior director was not stopping me from attending he signed for me to go on the trip. I had until noon to get all of my paperwork in to the office. After I forward my information and the senior director's approval. The fake trip to Texas was cancelled.

01.11.16. I could not find the name of the person who sent the email in the company directory. The person who cancelled the trip stated he was a contractor that worked out of the site location and that is why no one knows him at the headquarters. Let's see if I get a follow up email in Mid-year. More than likely the same time as my annual other organization trip. Not that I am surprised the trip was supposedly cancelled due to a mix up with the number of people requested to attend. Can we guest who was cut from the list? As of date of this book March 1, 2018 I still have not heard back concerning the Texas trip. I also would like to mention that the Dallas trip is a trip from affiliate of the company for minority employees. This is a different trip from when I mention Texas.

02.22.16 Deemon Monstah is still allowed to delete and alter emails and other documents.

04.06.16 Stole my work ID again and threatened to take my car keys and purse. My recommendation is instead of stealing let's all go to the Justice Department. This can be resolved by having the Justice Department from Washington, DC come and investigate the misuse of federal funds to terrorize African American employees.

04.18.16 Deemon is still allowed to continue the harassment with technology with the approval and assistance of Mitch Holden. Today, Deemon changed a subject heading on an email that I sent out to POM organization. In addition, to the junk mail that was sent to my house mostly insurance for death benefits, which is their standard line of terrorism, I am constantly receiving threats. Moreover, the continuation of illegally tampering with electric and water bill to increase.

As previously stated when you see gaps in the chronological sections it is because Deemon Monster is illegally tampering in other areas of my life such as my ministry, my finances, my family and steadily finding means and ways to violate my privacy.

08.17.16 Mitch Holden is still allowing Deemon Monstah to have control over my computer. This morning I was unable to log on using my password. I am requesting that all cords that connect my computer to Deemon's be disconnected. The abuse of tampering with the emails and delete company information and now not being able to log on is enough of Deemon's foolishness, abuse of company resources and time. The purpose of this is to make it difficult for me working so I will quit. Unfortunately, because Deemon is not skilled or knowledgeable in my position he is unable to accomplish his goal. Again, disconnect his computer and technical power and you will disconnect the problem source.

11.15.16 Back in July because I was granted to go to POM National in Dallas a professional development conference similar to what my white colleagues do all the time with no conflict. I suffered retaliation from Deemon because I am an African American female and Deemon feels that I should not have equal rights within this division and company. He has done and is doing every illegal act to take away money from me. One of the things done with Governor Harvey Fetter's approval, Mitch and Capt. Linden was to have my daughter stopped in Virginia with a fake speeding ticket. Virginia is one of the toughest states to receive a speeding ticket.

12.19.16 My vacation slip was turned in on Friday, December 16, 2016 at 9:34 am. The norm is to place my vacation slip in my mailbox after I have taken the vacation time. I am unable to receive my signed vacation slip like my other co-workers.

12.16.16 I received the email notice about work PC Replacement on 12.15.16. What good is PC Replacement going to do Deemon can use his position as Senior Director to still control and manipulate my computer? On numerous occasions, my layout configuration has been changed. Emails deleted or changed, attachments deleted or changed. Emails have been added. Typos that I did not make were added to the emails that I sent out. Emails were sent using my name that I did not send. Unless the Company is planning on disconnecting Deemon from my computer and stopping the Homeland Security abuse the PC Replacement is a waste.

Children Abuse

As previously stated the vile and vicious attacks were not just against me, but also against my children and grandchildren as well on every level emotionally, psychologically, financially and physically. Furthermore, because of my spiritual background it gave me stability and therefore, The Company police at the request of Deemon Monstah decided to attach my sweet innocent grandchildren the unsuspecting. I have three granddaughters and one grandson in this state. I have another granddaughter in Texas which he constantly threatens to have her harm.

One of the reasons for the attack on the children is to damage their teeth. As Deemon Monstah has a genetic heredity flaw in his family with bad teeth and have had dental reconstructive surgery with all teeth removed and replaced he despised me for my nice smile that I am complimented on daily. Moreover, he seizes the opportunity to tamper with my daughter's dental and health insurance via computer to have them temporarily without insurance to cause the children to not to be able to go to the dentist.

12.31.15 On New Year's Eve, I went to church and my older grandchildren were at home. The selected few police officers were terrorizing my grandchildren by keep knocking on door at house. The children were so terrified that the mother had to come and pick them up from the house. Furthermore, because of my spiritual background, it gave me endurance to survive in these attacks. So, the new tactic was to attack my area of weak links, my grandchildren. The company police attacked the innocent and unsuspecting children.

01.14.16 The company police stole my granddaughter's Science book. The reason the police stole the book was to cause and economic injustice. The police just like Deemon believed if he could exhaust my finances and exhaust me. I would submit as their slave.

02.22.16 The company police used the technology to tap into my grandson nervous system in school and impact his cognitive behavior.

03.02.16 Yesterday the company police used technology again to stop clocks at my home so that my grandson would miss school. The alarm did not ring as scheduled.

03.23.16 This was another day the police kept grandson from going to school using the biological warfare influencing his cognitive behavior.

04.01.16 Used technology to tap into State system and tamper with my daughter's social service benefits for her to obtain food benefits for the children. Another terroristic tactic of harming innocent African American children by starvation. This is a form of genocide to the African race. Imagine if this is done to all single mothers in the state.

04.22.16 My grandson was sent home from school due to the biological warfare used on him. Nurse believed it to be ringworm patch, but it turned out to be rash when sent to the doctor. The goal is to keep my grandson out school. A black male is seen as a threat.

04.26.16 My access was denied to print the kindergarten form for my granddaughter to attend school in the fall. Political influence was used to have my grandson seen by school psychologist for anger management when in fact it is Deemon Monstah that has the anger management issue. This is his cry for help. Has anyone looked at Deemon Monstah's psychological records? Or had him examined psychologically?

04.27.16 Deemon Monstah illegally is tampering with grandchildren's school records via technology by placing negative and harmful information to impact and influence poor decision making concerning children's grades and placement. Causing one granddaughter to be possibly redistrict from attending the same school as brother. I shall request that all records that contain falsified negative and harmful information be expunged. I have written to the Board of Education and shared both lawsuits with them. It is my hopes that the decision is made to get rid of these people for illegally using the technology against African Americans children.

05.02.16 The company police with approval from Deemon and Mitch is still using technology to steal documents and grandchildren's homework. Because Deemon has failed tests all his life such as the bar exam, he is acting out by tampering with my grandchildren's school work. He is threatened by me because of the degrees and awards I have achieved.

05.03.16 The company police hit my daughter's car while we were on our way to my grandson school because I wanted to show that the school documents were tampered with and I had a letter I was going to submit.

05.09.16 Threaten to stop my granddaughter from attending kindergarten in the fall by delaying paperwork electronically.

05.09.16 Threatening to have one granddaughter be retained because of technology in removing documents in book bag and hiding work assignments.

12.07.16 The hatred of me advancing in any area is still a major issue with Deemon. Moreover, because he is allowed to abuse the Homeland Security technology and monitor my finances and my daughter's to continuously cause hardships to cost me money. The economic injustice that this person has been allowed to do is unbelievable in a land supposedly of freedom. My daughter's tire was flattened this morning causing her to have to withdraw money from my account and pay an ATM withdrawal fee. While I budget to move ahead since I am being discriminated against by not being promoted or upgraded in this company. Deemon hates the idea of me having money and able to save while he causes unnecessary expenses for me and my family. The illegal technology is still being used for the water bill and electric bill.

12.15.16 Even after I submitted the harassment, discrimination and retaliation complaint to EEO I am still being harassed. As previously stated, my home computer, printer and cell phone has been blacked out due to the illegal use of Homeland Security. Because of the technology used they can manipulate documents and place them anywhere. This is just another terroristic tactic. Stating they found my documents on the printer and picked up by mistake.

12.19.16 On Friday, December 16, 2016 Homeland Security technology was used to lock me in my car at the store Five Below while my older grandchildren were in the store. In 2013, the company police broke into my house and stole the car manual book along with other documents this was reported to the Township Police. As part of their continued conspiracy of harassment and retaliation, the purpose was to intimidate me for reporting their domestic terroristic acts in my recent EEO complaint on December 14, 2016. This excessive punishment and hate crime is an example of their past performances of abuse of their positions, technology and police force.

12.21.16 I received a Motor Vehicle Commission letter asking me to pay a fee of $85 and sign my vehicle over with the title. It is Deemon's belief that I should not have anything. While I manage to budget and save money despite not receiving equal pay for equal work because I am an African American female.

12.27.16 The constant abuse of our federal dollars continues. As false documents are prepared to steal my house and my car. The latest is a letter from the credit union asking me to sign my vehicle over to the credit union.

01.31.17 The use of blocking my home computer, printer and personal cell phone is still in effect. I am unable to forward my Liberty Mutual Insurance information and to forward information to Great Lakes for my student loan. This is crucial as each day this cost me money with interest and Deemon in his psychotic bipolar state has determined that I am to have nothing and will go to great lengths to ensure that I lose money in any capacity.

02.15.17 The retaliation continues as chemical warfare tactics via NeuroScience were used on me on Sunday, February 12 and Monday, February 13 as well as continued threats of falsifying my signature and stealing my car.

02.24.17 The terrorizing with the threats continues with the threat of using biological warfare and neuroscience to have me get sick at work so they may have an excuse to have me carried out in an ambulance and require that I see their doctor upon return. I am healthy and fine. Any illness is because of any chemical that is placed at my desk or the use of biological warfare. Deemon has done both of these in the past.

03.06.17 I am still requesting the review of the technology capability of the Homeland Security purchases here at the company.

03.17.17 The threats keep occurring about taking my life or doing bodily harm to me. This time with my blood and lab work that I need to have done. Everything is done via technology so tests can be manipulated to state whatever they want to state. Medication is then prescribed for an illness that does not exist based on a tampered with technological test results. Again, I asked the question has anyone read the Technology capability in the Father Documents. Board Members signed off on these documents. Do they know what they were signing?

03.24.17 Another vicious cyber terroristic attack with home computer, printer, and personal cell phone. Continued threats of illegally tampering with town's tax assessment for home and increase in my car insurance. Sending enormous DMV amounts for false ticket given in Virginia during a racial profile stop by one of their racist police associate. All this is authorized and approved by former Governor Harvey Fetter. The former Governor can be reported for his approval and authorization of these terroristic cybercrimes. This makes the company and its representatives' accomplices and look incompetent in doing their jobs, therefore liable for whatever happens.

03.27.17 As the demon control the terrorizing continues with the illegal use of technology and the former Governor's involvement, I now have to address Identity Theft and credit report issues.

04.06.17 The threats keep occurring as it is represented by the company and the state. I personally hold the former Governor Harvey Fetter accountable for everything that has happened as he has allowed this to continue.

My older brother was previously struck by a bus which was no coincidence; let's hope the same incident is not in the design for me. Also, let the record reflect that while The Company was illegally tampering with computer records of mine they were also tampering with my family's records as well.

With threats of tampering with my grandchildren's grades and their education, I am preparing to share all necessary information with the Board of Education, the state Teachers Association and Washington, DC Dept. of Education. This Synapse Gap and illegal use of technology has got to stop. When will The Company and the Board of Directors stop this terrible atrocity? It is bad enough that these Domestic Terrorists have used technology to control human beings in this human trafficking of invasion of privacy and thoughts. With this technology, the

Justice Department now needs to look at all arrests concerning African Americans since having this technology. How many cases of entrapment have been used to get rid of African American the company employees? Evidence has already shown that there is a collation between filing an EEO Complaint and then being sent to Employee Assistance Program (EAP).

In the continuing racial disparity, this company is a member of the Minority National Organization and has discontinued paying its annual membership dues. This will cause a hardship for the African American employees at this company that would like to attend the annual conference. Being that the president of our local chapter is in the middle of discrimination lawsuit, this is another intentional act of racial discrimination. Why are the other national organizational dues paid and not the minority organization? This confirms the truth written in most EEO cases and discrimination lawsuits that the company is detrimental to African Americans career development and advancement. Here at this company when they block such programs as the national minority organizations this is designed to give information for career development and advancement.

04.06.17 With the illegal use of technology a cyber or medical attack can occur at any time. I was just threatened with receiving a fever sore because of what I wrote yesterday. This is because I mentioned yesterday about the synapse gap they can send signals to the brain which causes natural body functions to react. What they believe is their most ardent threat of sending me to EAP. As they were able to get away with this in the past by having Captain Linden Weeks lie and sign a document to send me to medical. What ever happen to the Police Report? How many African American females will The Company send to EAP for filing an EEO case?

All of this will be brought out when the Federal Justice Department do they investigation. They are familiar with the technology and the medical advances as previously stated that was given as a preventive measure against terrorism but is now being used as part of domestic terroristic attacks and hate crimes. The constant threat to African Americans includes the church where I currently pastor with such things as fake animal sounds and tampering with the water, fuel and electricity bill. All under the approval and authorization of the former Governor Fetter at the recommendation of Deemon Monstah who mimic what was done at the Crossover Tunnel and who was hired and knowingly lied on his resume and if a police background check was done they would know he also have a police record for lewd behavior. As you continue to read this book you will see that his lewd behavior surfaces throughout this book in his invasion of privacy crimes and aggressive behavior through technology.

04.05.17 The new threat is to call a meeting with me and use the technology university velocity method combined with the illegal University Medical Research with Synapse Gap to cause me to fall. With the company witnesses, I would be forced to stay out of work until I see a University Research Scientist. Please tell me what is the urgency of me seeing the University Scientist? Hasn't the Company done enough experiments on African Americans?

I am now being harassed via my home phone constantly ringing. I am still receiving continuous threats of having medical testing done by the University Medical Research team and allowing the abusers of the company police to enter my home. Again, I want to state I am not going to allow those scientists to do any type of medical testing. I am not allowing company police to enter my home. I have blocked all windows and doors except the front door. It my hopes that this matter be turned over to the Federal Justice Department. The select few at the company are criminals without a shadow of a doubt.

Again, I state they cannot be trusted and should not be policing themselves. We need federal intervention. The former Governor Harvey Fetter is not only involved but is the approver. It is no way this would be able to continue under the watch of the former Governor Fetter and he not be involved. There is a mess here at The Company with The Advertising Company, Little Rock Consulting Firm, Technology Institute and the University Research Team. The Father Document was approved by The Company Board who has the former Governor Representatives on the Board. The State and The Company will be responsible for not taking any action to resolve this matter. First and foremost, by firing Deemon Monstah who wants the position as the lead and is the lead coconspirator and the main agitator. Deemon Monstah has turned a racial discrimination case into a personal vendetta. The evidence is clear and convincing this is a Hate Crime. Deemon Monstah has done exactly what the former Governor Harvey Fetter did at Crossover Tunnel. Deemon mimic everything the Governor Fetter did in his office down to the titles and phony positions with high pay. The Chief of Staffs, the positions of the internal executive people involved as well as the select few company police officers Captain Linden Weeks and IT CFO Holden Mitch.

04.11.17 It was brought to my attention that the illegal tampering of the banking is still ongoing. The latest is my daughter and my joint saving account. It was closed in January and Deemon with the former Governor's approval had it open again with money being taking from the saving's account to the checking account costing us money. Twenty-five dollars a month was transferred to a cyber account. You would think with the scandal of Crossover Tunnel and the Synapse Gap with University Medical Research and Technology Institute that they would not have time to keep the racial profile of harassing me. I receive the encrypted message of the sad fact that the stealing from me helps pay for the harassment of me. I had $25 a month going into a Roth Account. The monthly payment has been stopped and I am not allowed to continue making electronic payments. I have to physically go into the bank to make a payment.

According to the Discovery review in my discrimination lawsuit Deemon Monstah made several recommendations for me to be fired despite my outstanding record prior to his arrival to this company. Today, I am making the same recommendation of him that he be fired for all the illegal activity done to my family and me. While firing Deemon will not bring back my brother or right the wrongs he has done, it is a start to begin fixing the damage he has done and to stop the chaos.

I want to go back to around October 2013, to mention Deemon showing me the Groucho Marx photo and mentioning the structure, key players and being strategically placed. That meeting at that time is the turning point, however, I did not realize although I remember it. Deemon thought at that time he had defeated me, so he revealed his plan. Deemon revealed the components of his devious plan which was governance, structure and the support of key players that have been strategically placed. His monologue was actually said to me the day after I withdrew my discrimination case. This all makes sense now. The plan he had in place from 2011 was cold and calculated. This is nothing short than <u>premediated murder</u> that was meant for me but instead happened to my brother. The terrorizing was still continuing with the emails, the texts, the biological warfare and the house break-ins.

In reflection, Deemon Monstah shared the **PACK** that was made between him and the others. I will share more details of the **PACK** in Chapter Six. Deemon Monstah was comparing himself to Groucho Marx who was American comedian, writer, stage film, and radio and television star. He was known as a master of quick wit. One of the reasons Deemon wanted me out of my position was I oversaw the Film Program and articles would be in The Company paper, magazines and newspaper about my work. I was The Company representative in that area and he hated that fact. He hated it so much that he made the recommendation to abolish filming for The Company altogether although it was generating additional revenue. He had all my company phones call and emails go to him.

04.11.17 Over the weekend the terroristic tactics continued using Homeland Security anti-terrorism tactics. With the illegal use of the Synapse Gap and electronic frequency I received a pain starting in the left foot initiating in to cramp. In addition, because of the self-identity issue and insecurity of Deemon I have also receive threats of leg amputations. He likes to wear women's clothing but have not mastered the three-inch heels which I wear all the time.

04.13.14 My cell phone has been literally buzzing and as in the past it is Blacked Out. This is a notorious pattern whenever they fear that I may have contact with someone who will assist in exposing the invasion of privacy and violation of my constitutional rights for their illegal medical tapping in the Synapse Gap the select few will black out my phone. I will continue to fight for my constitutional rights and freedom. In addition, the engineered fall, the leg amputation, ambulance, and emergency room visit threat is still ongoing. You would think with the Crossover Tunnel incident and the Father Document Communication Agreements they would LEAVE ME ALONE!!! Hopefully, they have not changed the Father Document from what the Board of Directors have already approved in 2012. This is all at the recommendation of Deemon Monstah and the approval of former Governor Harvey Fetter.

04.12.17 Up until the last second Deemon Monstah continues his harassment from delaying the traffic light at 4pm allowing several people to miss their commute to having the bus reroute to cause an even greater delay. Traffic Lights are controlled by computers so interrupting the signal is not an issue but causing traffic jams are. Again, this how Harvey Fetter allows our tax dollars to be spent. Currently, Deemon with assistance of company Police Officers Linden Weeks and Wyner Punster team has had my cell phone turned completely off. Who tracks the illegal usage of these technological decisions?

One of Deemon's childish ways is not signing my vacation slip. I am used to having my vacation form not signed until after I return or ask for it. This is another one of his demented power plays for me to ask him for something or his permission. Because of his unstable, diabolical scheming, and low self-esteem, I stay as far away from Deemon as much as possible. Deemon on the other had finds every possible means to see me. I intentionally walk the long way around to keep from going past his office. Deemon then claims to have a question for my co-worker so that he can enter into my work space. I keep my back turned because I do not want to look at him. Deemon has access to my calendar and phone and knows when I leave my cubicle so he intentionally stands and waits for me to walk by him. If I speak with the secretary, he comes out of his office with supposedly a question for her. Please I walk away all the time. I cannot even stand in the hall and speak with co-workers as Deemon will walk towards us to start interrupt and start speaking. Again, as I notice Deemon is headed in my direction I leave quickly.

05.05.17 With all of this happening with technology the biopsychology which is a branch of psychology interested in discovering the biological bases of our thoughts feelings and behavior. Back in 2013, I received a request for Cognitive behavior study on a cell tower. Because it is known that the human neurons which are communicating cell and dendrites which carry information to a cell in the body can now be used via technology of cell towers and structures. By structures I am referring to axon terminals in the human body which are structure at the end of axon that contain transmitter substances. In the human body the myelin sheath which is the speed of conducting an action potential is very rapid in neurons possessing a myelin sheath. The Graded Potential is important. Researchers have identifying drugs to alter synaptic transmission for practical purposes. Unfortunately, addictions and mental disorders can occur from this. The synaptic transmission that occurs in human beings is the key. The synaptic transmission is the axon terminals found on the ends of axon contain many synaptic vesicles. When an action potential reaches the axon terminal, these vesicles move toward the cell membrane. Once there the vesicles fuse with the membrane and release their contents neurotransmitters.

In other words, an electrical signal can be converted to a chemical signal in our bodies. So, a computer can send a signal to humans and control their cognitive behavior such as thoughts, feelings and behaviors. I am administrator who handles communication contracts and the process. I know my job!

The plan now is to continue to manipulate my schedule, caused unnecessary confusion with documents I need to transact business such as my mortgage statement and diplomas, and to drain me financially with interest fees, late fees and all sorts of other electronic ways to steal money from me. Deemon holds my personal checks I write in cyber space for weeks and or months before releasing them to be deposit. When I originally found out I was purchasing money orders. However, this becomes costly and in addition, if he holds the mail I may end up having to hand-deliver which is not always an option. Deemon also does the same for the church checks. He continuously adds unnecessary fees on bills for both my personal home and the church. Deemon holds bills and changes the billing dates. Deemon does all of these things to cripple me financially.

05.22.17 The latest Harvey Fetter approval given to allow Deemon to continue this domestic terrorism was to increase my daughter's utility bills; use the Cognitive Behavior technology against my granddaughter in school, along with members of the church; removing my granddaughter's books to cause financial hardship in replacing them. Causing a car accident with Tammy Sweets to have her vehicle totaled and threaten to do the same to me. The cybercrimes still occurring with encrypted phone calls, emails and texts. I am not sure why the pressing urge to enter my home, but those threats are increasing. There is absolutely no reason for the company police to enter my home. They are trying every tactic and maneuver from fake utility person to cable personnel to roofer. Now Deemon is issuing the threat of having a fake warrant for searching my home. When will the Federal Government step in and stop this culprits from abusing their positions and violating constitutional rights.

06.05.17 While I have not been documenting every single act former Governor Harvey Fetter have been allowing Deemon to do it has been the same such as traffic delays; near car accidents, continuing death threats, threats of setting my house on fire and breaking into my home. The latest of his demented ways impacts the elderly which should be noted. As it is known that the University Medical Research illegal use of tapping into the synapse gap and doing illegal experiments on African Americans with the cell tower and central nervous system. These domestic terrorists are attacking the seniors at my church. Deemon believes I should not have anything and he finds ways and means to steal money from my family, my friends and me all the time. He stole $50 from my mother's money with the technology of separating particles of matter. To a senior $50 is a lot of money while he thinks it is funny. The latest is the funds at the church where I pastor. We had a budget and it was working out very well. Deemon because he is petty, weak, and jealous has increased the utilities, gas bill and insurance causing an unnecessary hardship on elderly members. The orders given from former Governor Harvey Fetter are to lean hard on me as tactic and escalate the threats and the financial burden. Little does he know this tactic does not work instead it inspires and encourages me to continue to do the right thing and fight for social justice.

06.06.17 There is a street light by the corner of my home in which I have lived there for almost twenty years. The streetlight has never been out. Ignorance outweighs safety yet again in this domestic violence. Someone can fall and get hurt trying to walk from the landing to the parking lot. The purpose of the light is because the area used to be woods and now the complex was developed. At night fall it is pitch dark. I have my grandchildren and elderly parents who visit me. If Deemon's purpose was to scare and intimidate me, he failed miserably. However, if it is to show his level of desperation in his personal vendetta against me and my family with Harvey Fetter's authorization, he has proven once again that his personal attacks are not well thought out and it is blatantly obvious of his illegal use again of technology.

07.11.17 Deemon Monstah using technology again and was able to delay my regular scheduled bus on the No. 25 on yesterday July 10, 2017 to stop in front of the Dollar Store. The plan as previously stated is to force me to sign an illegal unethical agreement for a fake position to work in Acquisition Appropriations (AA). Acquisition Appropriations has been in several class action discrimination lawsuits and outside of the company police department leads the way for the racial discrimination at the company. Deemon wants me to report to one of his associates who have plans to harass me until I retire or quit. The so-called promotion is a low level fake manager's position that will rely on the computer in which they will have control of to start the write ups of poor workmanship and errors. I have declined on numerous times that I am not interested in any of their diabolical illegal and unethical scams.

07.11.17 Because the control of the nervous system and the cabling with communication. I was given a threat that my father will need a walker. I just found out that last night my father was taken to the emergency and given a walker. Deemon is jealous of the relationship that I have with my father. My parents are proud of what I have accomplished, despite the racist opposition. This is the type illegal unethical practice I have to deal with the select few and Homeland Security is doing in the state.

Biological warfare was used on my older sister who is a diabetic and she was placed in the Hospital with severe abdominal pains (due to technology referenced in Chapter Three) in Hospital. Officer Wyner Punkster, Deemon and Mitch Holden were allowed to cause havoc for her while she was in the hospital on or around October 28, 2017. Deemon is continuing illegal tampering with checking account and the removing overdraft protection from my bank account.

11.07.17 I am leaving in a few days for Philadelphia. I received threats that my home will be broken into while I away. I have gone to the police station in my town after receiving the threat and the police was waiting for me at the Township Police Station. The normal process is to ask for identification, accept the Citizen Complaint form and assign a number to complaint. In addition, there was normally one of two officers in the room. The night I went to the reception desk there were five or six officers. One officer stated there was no need to neither accept my Citizen Complaint nor assign me a number. This is standard process to alert police when you are going out of town. The officer did not allow me to state my purpose for being there instead just wanted my address and was interested in I had an alarm on the house. I filled out the form and left the Citizen Complaint in the window where the police normally accept complaints.

11.13.17 One would think that a person would stop the threats now with everything at the surface and the truth being told. However, that is not the case. Technology still is being illegally used such as tampering with the traffic lights, the GPS device, the cell phone and the continuous changing of documents to have typos on them.

11.22.17 Tampering with the nonprofit 501 c 3 form for the women's organization I formed by deleting attachments, and now by delaying the process by holding the document in cyberspace. The vehicles threat of my daughter's and my car transmission because I am aware of what Fetter is doing with the synaptic transmission.

11.21.17 The new threat of having my daughter falsely arrested to use as pressure to have me stop the lawsuit of the violation of my constitutional and human rights against Harvey Fetter. The false ticket given in Virginia is still being sent to <u>extort money from my daughter</u>. In addition, to the continuous tickets in town along with a two-year surcharge of $42 a month. All of these tactics are per Harvey Fetter and will not work. I am still going to tell the truth.

11.21.17 The company police officers are still tampering with the US Post Office mail. My daughter mailed her medical insurance documents and they had it returned to her to delay the process of medical benefits for her and the children just as they did my brother.

I am still dealing with the ongoing threat of tampering with my heating system unit outside of my house along with them placing several mouse traps near my basement window.

12.01.17 Despite the illegal tampering with my bank account, I still manage to pay all my bills and have money saved. I am denied access to view my Credit Union account online. I have to physically go to the bank to see balances, make transactions and transfer money in between accounts. Today, I was denied access to the ATM located at The Company headquarters. The reason for the denial of access to my bank account is to cause an inconvenience and to have me have to pay a bank fee to go somewhere else to withdraw money. In addition, my timesheet balance has been tampered with and altered. This is all at the direction of the Harvey Fetter harassment and retaliation. I am constantly reminded that Deemon Monstah's goal is to drain my family and me of every possible penny. Once these criminal acts are exposed everything with my accounts will be cleared and corrected.

12.21.17 As the evil behavior indicates these are cruel vicious creatures that continuously use racism and abuse of Homeland Security technology with the approval authorization of former Governor Harvey Fetter. As previously mentioned my home was broken into and my vehicle a few years back when this illegal constitutional conspiracy was conceived. Outside of documents stolen from my home, I had my vehicle manual and quick reference car book on the list of items stolen. My vehicle as with most vehicles is computerized so they have the frequency and technology to interfere with my vehicle controls. Currently, they have programmed the vehicle to shut off, they have lights turn on and off, and roll the windows down. In addition, they can send a false reading to the car needs repair when it does not. The purpose of the false reading is because I managed, sacrificed and budgeted to save up money. Deemon is passionate about his goal to have me in a financial bind so that I may be desperate to except their crooked unethical and illegal business offer. They are looking for me to sign a <u>consent form and confidentiality statement</u>. I am **NOT** signing either one of them. Deemon sits in his office while on the phone and repeats these words. I know and I will take care of it. This is the lie he tells as he continues to escalate and commit more crimes which has brought him to this point.

12.26.17 I was given a threat because I wanted to exercise my right to freedom of Speech and Freedom of Religion. The threat was on shutting my car off. I had my car checked out and it is fine. On Friday, I am supposed to give Christmas baskets with turkey and trimmings to families. On Saturday I am scheduled to visit my Parents. Sunday I am preaching about Truth and the Shepherds spreading the Good News at another church. This lets me know I am telling the Truth because Fetter wants to stop me from speaking. I am not against Homeland Security technology. I am against people like Fetter illegally using Homeland Security technology to retaliate with Domestic Terrorism against African Americans.

12.27.17 Since I reported the threat against my vehicle on 12.21.17 I instead was attacked on Sunday, December 24, 2017 via biological warfare causing nausea, fainting spells, body aches and headaches. All signals that can be sent electronically to the body causing the body to react to the false symptoms. This is also reasons I was out of the office on 12.26.17 to recuperate from the false illness. One of the dangers of this is having people take medication they do not need for symptoms they really do not have which in turn causes even more damage. In addition, because a fever sore is a virus they can have it erupt at any time, so I was given one. The purpose of making me ill on Sunday was to prevent me from preaching my sermon and connecting with the local pastor in the community. While I pressed my way and preached the local pastor had a staged car accident the select few caused to delay him from being at the church and hearing me preach. I know this was no coincidence. Thank heaven, no one was hurt.

Furthermore, their cruel monstrous nature is still tampering with my emails. They pulled up an old yahoo email address so that I would not receive emails from people and miss out of religious appointments. I am still unable to use my personal laptop and printer. In addition, I have been denied access to my student loan and unable to make a payment via computer or telephone to cause an increase in interest being added. I am also denied access to my credit union to review balances and make transactions. So, I have to physically go into the bank.

Biological Warfare Medical Technology Abuse

03.16.16. My grandson was targeted for biological terroristic attack with diarrhea because he was a black male and related to me. He had to miss another day of school.

03.21.16 Yesterday, with the illegal medical technology from University Research and the technology institute the physics of having my five-year-old granddaughter fall out of the car and also push her onto the ground. These were two separate fall incidents. Have anyone looked into the federal grants of the Medical Research performing illegal medical acts along with The Technology Institute.

04.28.16 Biological warfare is being used today on my hands to feel frozen. In addition, to causing hot and cold flashes, my eyes to tear unnecessarily and the threat of hitting me in the eyes I still came to work. I am now receiving threats that the select few plan to use the University Medical technology to have my granddaughter sleep walk. When will the ties between The University Medical technology and their illegal medical testing be investigated?

05.19.16 With Cognitive Data Dispatch the experimentation is utilizing frequencies to interrupt and interfere with normal cognitive behavior functions such as eye twitching, nervousness. It masks your normal behavior because your normal signal is interrupted.

07.07.16 My prescription medication was stolen from mail. My regular medical doctor was switched to force me to see a University owned medical doctor. Lab results are computerized and have been altered as another reason to see University owned medical doctor. This is a Health Fraud.

08.02.16 Another work tactic used is the stigmatization of forcing someone to go to Medical for no reason or a made-up reason out of so-called concern in order to have racial control. This is a blatant misuse of Corporate Policy to authorize and to legalize discriminatory actions against me. This was done in 2012 and the questions to that policy as of date still where not addressed. I wanted to share the questions in this book, but the questions were stolen. The questioned at in my EEO complaint were never addressed.

08.02.16 I just found out that the billing for my Express Scripts has been tampered with and the 1-800 number to call customer service has been diverted to a person referring me to file a police report.

11.09.16 Homeland Security continues the illegal Wiretap into personal calendar: Please note the consistent changes in requestor's date requests to coincide with dates in my calendar.

11.15.16 University Research Medical group in conjunction with Homeland Security and Technology University has been allowed to use chemical warfare against me. Again, I ask for this list of items purchased for Homeland Security and the side agreements for this joint venture.

03.17.17 The threats keep occurring and this time with my blood and lab work that I need to have done. Everything is done via technology, so tests can manipulate to state whatever they want to state. Medication is then prescribed for an illness that does not exist based on a tampered with technological test results. Again, I asked the question has anyone read the Technological Father Documents. Board Members signed off on these documents. Do they know what they were signing?

03.21.17 I am now receiving threats of the terrorists coming into my house again I will alert the township police and my neighbors of any suspicious activity around my home. Currently, with the technology the police have access in using every meeting I have is intentionally doubled-booked.

While the following issue is still a prevalent matter in the work place so is the continued abuse of power with fake work request. I took the time to share the unveiling of the technology discovery to save a life. My brother lost his life because of the abuse of power given to a select. I am trying to prevent another loss of life. The selected few cut his food, his social services benefits, communication and other resources. This is a slow and agonizing death. As each one of my family members went through this process in some way shape or form, one of us did not make it. One of the reasons was because he was in another state and due to all our extenuating circumstances, we were all suffering at the time; we could not get to him. I pray this information reaches the right hands to help someone who may be experiencing what I have gone through. I know I have shared and suffered some dehumanizing experiences as racism tried to use genocide of a race and enslave me. However, this is not just about me it is a crime against humanity. It was me today, but it can be someone else tomorrow that they do not like because they have the power and the position and use it illegally.

Chapter Four

No Justice

*I will open my mouth in parables;
I will utter things kept secret
from the foundation of the world.
Matthew 13:34-35 NKJV[iii]*

How did you endure the many afflictions trampled upon you? I reflected on the scripture in II Timothy 2:3-5, *"Thou therefore endure hardness, as a good soldier of Jesus Christ."* I then thought of slavery times as our fore parents that were chained to the bottom of the ships for months packed like sardines. I thought about the beatings given to runaway slaves and the many lynchings that were done, I thought about the riots of how the water hose of cold water was sprayed on our people, I thought about the feeling of what men felt like to be called boy or a grown woman to be called girl. They endured hardness as a good soldier of Jesus Christ and survived. Did it hurt? Yes! Was it degrading? Yes! To be treated less than human and have to come to work every day knowing the Truth about whom they really are. There are no more sheets to be worn. Today, they hide behind technology. At least in the past, you could pull the sheet back. Now, if racist is strategically placed in positions you cannot even go to the police.

When we look at The Company Affirmative Action Plan statistics they lump all minorities together in some instances they include white women who makes the statistics not look so bad. But when you peel back the layers and compare African American to other minorities the figures do not lie. African Americans are the lowest paid and have the lowest positions title in comparison to whites. Those that have been fortunate to be promoted to manager are low level managers making a $10,000 less than their similarly situated coworkers do. When you look at the job descriptions most of the time the African Americans are doing more work, been in The Company longer, and have the most experience. If you review the resumes, the original resumes submitted by a white colleague and the revised resume done by the senior director when he wants to place a white person or non-black into a position you will see a vast difference in the two resumes.

At this juncture, I wanted to stress that I am not stating this is the situation for all white resumes submitted nor am I stating this for all white supervisors. I myself was fortunate prior to 2008 to have had good supervisors who were all white and who were predominately male.

As I introduced myself in the first chapter and begin to share my story I intentionally left out the description the senior director so that you may form your own opinion of him. I while at this time share my perception based on the horrible experiences I have in dealing with this individual. The senior director is incoherent, confusing and disoriented. His thoughts are not clear. Read his emails. He complains of my grammar, but he does not use complete sentences. I originally thought that it was intentionally to cover him legally, but now after thinking about it he may be that he is not capable of writing a complete sentence.

What I am up against and have to deal with every single day is a middle age racist white man who is divorced who is named Deemon Monstah. One of the split personalities is in love with the CFO of IT Mitch Holden. Whenever Deemon gets into technical trouble he calls on Mitch to bail him out the trouble. Mitch is an enabler for Deemon. While Deemon has a very low self-esteem of himself he makes Mitch be his super hero. He secretly despises Mitch for his gifts, talents and computer knowledge, but because he needs him he also loves what Mitch can do for him. This in turns feeds Mitch's ego because he has another so-called male that look up to him both intellectually and physically. As Deemon is not only short in temper, short in kindness and short in intellect and skills he is just short. While height is not an issue as I am only 5 feet 4 inches. Deemon constantly displays the Napoleon Complex and has an issue with his height.

Michael Jackson wrote a song entitled, Man in the Mirror. So, I am writing about the man in the mirror. It is time that he be unmasked and stop hiding behind other people and technology. Deemon is known as dream killer because he did not pass the bar exam and he now wants to crush other people's dream. He likes to wear women's clothes. He is schizophrenic with multiple personalities. One of his personalities is jealous of me as an African American female employee at work. He mimics my life from my clothes to my make-up. Women can tell when other women wear make-up or when your nails have been painted. I realize with science that we have artificial intelligence. I also know there is the technology to make phone calls seem like they are coming from various areas and they are not. This is something that Deemon likes to do on a regular basis and the company police allow him this technology and to harass me. He does the same thing with emails and the company police allow him to do that as well. He also has a genetic birth defeat because of the incest in the family. He wants to be revered as a genius but failed the bar exam, lied on his resume and stole from The Company.

As it stands now, I need the assistance of the world knowing what is happening. They are trying to back me in the corner. In a criminal case, when have you heard of a victim ever being forced to negotiate with perpetrator? I am threatened every day all day to negotiate with the select few in an illegal contract. I will stand strong. I receive messages from the select few wanting to meet with me alone without an attorney. The demented want me to deal with the devil. For one million dollars, a promotion to a low-level manager, but I will be placed under another racist supervisor and a meager $10,000 a year increase they will consider the matter solved. Keep in mind, the invasion of privacy would still continue. Let's see they have tampered with my 401 K, my checking account, my credit report, my medical records, my student loan and the same for my daughter. They will continue to use Homeland security and invade my privacy and life. They want all my documents and evidence. We all know what will happen after I give them everything.

In addition, they are stealing from me electronically what is going to stop them from taking whatever they offer to me. I have lost so much money already. What happen to Federal investigation and trial? They believe strongly that they are above the law. If the federal government can look at the proper procedures in this matter, it would make a huge difference. I currently have a videotape on my cell phone that I did in front of the Hall of Records and due to the illegally use of Homeland Security I am unable to send it via Facebook and to others because they do not want the truth out.

The original plan was to destroy me psychologically, educationally, mentally, emotionally and most of economically. They wanted me to be broken and I was supposed to serve as an example of what happens when you go against the regime. Instead, I grew spiritually! I am aware of Deemon and what he is and he uses his position to harass me.

So why continue in this struggle in this fight. Let's look at history to answer that question. What happened if they did fight against slavery? Fight for voting rights? Fight for education, housing and other equal rights. Thank you, Rev. Dr. Martin Luther King Jr., thank you Rosa Parks, thank you Medgar Evans, Tommie Smith, John Carlos, Harriet Tubman, Fredrick Douglass just give homage to a few. Malcolm X said it best, *"If not now than when, if not me then who?"* We as a people, as a nation should unite and stand. If I can pave the way for someone else not to experience what I have gone through these past teen years than my living is not in vain. Terrorists count on people being afraid and not standing up. Terrorists count on people getting tired in well-doing! If everyone does his part, we can change the world and make it a better place. I am not bitter, I am better. A select few law enforcement officers should serve without fear or favor. In this particular instance they serve to cause fear and give themselves favor at taxpayer's expense.

Further Abuses

Prior to December 15, 2015, I was keeping written notes of the abuses and due to the break-ins, the notes prior to this date were either stolen or misplaced. Below are abuses without the dates.

- University Medical Research Team performing Tuskegee Experiments on Black Children
- Continuing to steal money electronically out of Wells Fargo Brokerage account mutual fund account
- Generate fake letters/add computerized fees/send EZ photos/delay electronic payments sent
- Block calls & emails that are send and received
- Stole Jewelry from home
- Broke daughter's flat screen TV
- Broke daughter's cell phone envelop broken
- Broke and stole parent's items off moving truck
- Deleted or hide family photos
- Hit my car, daughter's car, niece's car, my nephew's car and friend's car
- Called with a fake refinance pretending to the bank that my car was finance on September 23 and company police placed a fee of $16.40 on my car bill
- Company police diverts all calls from my personal telephone

- Company police deleted job applications my daughter filled out on line. They also delete any appointments for job interviews.
- Destroyed cell phone device for charger
- Delaware claim for EZ Pass from July 2, 2011 keep sending bills and violations
- Personal disk & Church disk destroyed
- Company police sent a University check to me as a tuition refund for attending school because I believed it to be a scam I held the check as it came at a time when The Company police has attacked my finances in all areas. Two weeks later, I received a letter from the school stating it was a mistake and to please write a check for $2,020. My intuition was correct and it was a scam. When I went to return the check it was stolen. The school assisted that I replace the funds. I told the school to put a cancellation on the check as I never cashed it. That particular issue was resolved.
- The police have stolen my work phone. They also blocked my home computer to keep me from sending emails. How is illegally tampering with my phone and computer part of the Homeland Security.

01.14.16 Deemon increase typos in documents that I prepare and block the usage of the color printer.

01.24.16 Stole Driver's License. The purpose of stealing my identification is to cause me additional trouble and for me to incur the cost of replacing them. Habitual stealing.

01.22.16 Company Police used technology and stole my work pass.

01.22.16 The deleting of work and personal emails has continued.

03.29.16 My home television is blacked out when there are certain shows on television that The Company police do want me to view.

In 2016 The selected few are still using film and special events to convey threats to me. Please review chronological order and sections of emails and requests it will paint the picture for you. I received a threat on May 12, pertaining to my parked vehicle on the street.

09.07.16 In addition, they are still tampering with the US Postal mail which is a federal offense. I am still receiving countless offers for death benefits from various insurances along with medical insurance options for retirees.

10.18.16 I just received a voicemail message with my social security number as the return call. These are the type of threats I receive prior to some illegal activity being done such as Identity Theft with my social security number.

10.19.16 Via the illegal use of technology I was informed that I will not have use of my cell phone, laptop or any technology. I am encouraging everyone I speak to write their congress person pertaining to the illegal use of federal funds for personal racial vendettas and depriving me of my constitutional rights. How many African Americans have this illegal use of Homeland Security been used against? Washington needs to investigate the state starting with the Company Police.

More Work Abuses

01.13.16 The select few falsified my notary documents.
01.14.16 Deemon has increase typos in emailed documents, block usage of color printer.

03.11.16 My company cell phone is stolen. I was told I was excused from the ERT and then placed on the list to go to NY. The purpose is to cause undue stress and continue to make this a hostile work environment. Due to the financial hardship placed on my daughter because of illegal use of technology. Deemon knows I assist my daughter with the children. It was Deemon who has caused my daughter to lose her job. He operated on both ends. First, by having my daughter to have car trouble he initiated and then second by having her supervisor change her hours knowing with children it would be difficult to keep that schedule. In addition to the biological warfare with false symptoms to make her feel ill.

03.18.16 The select few are still tampering with my emails causing typos for Patricia to correct on Permits.

05.02.16 In addition, Deemon keeps stealing my cell phone accessories.

06.28.16 The trial is over and the terrorizing still continues. The Company police are tampering with the US Postal mail delaying membership to a company affiliation payment and my entry to an organization award. At this point, what I am to do. I cannot email, fax or mail anything without the police confiscating the item for Deemon. I know this is the goal to feel hopeless and helpless and to give in to their foul play. I will stand strong.

08.03.16 The virulent racism continues with diverting my personal cell phone call and personal email to my religious leadership by pretending to be a member of the staff. There is no "equal protection of the law" concerning the fraudulent abuse that a corrupted few is allowed to do. In addition to the stealing of my Minority Professional Organization membership payment out of the US Postal mail and removing my entry of nominating Minority Professional Organization online, I am still receiving the threat of IRS investigation. This abuse of the technology system guarantees discriminatory results. If you want proof read the Father Documents and follow the funds in Capital Planning. Those in the company that know what Deemon Monstah is doing and you do nothing to correct the situation make you an accessory to cybercrimes.

08.04.16 Received email warning that I will be unable to print using the color printer, may have other computer difficulties today, and would need to call the help desk. This tactic is normally done when I am caught up on my daily remedial tasks and have time to embark on a more suitable endeavor using creativity for the position. This is shunned upon because ideas and or suggestions that come from me are being denied and then resurface as someone's else such as Draft Strategy for Career Development.

08.04.16 Despite the inequality in this hostile work environment, I was given approval to go on the Minority Professional Organization National trip for career development and growth as my coworkers are also allowed to travel for business in their respective organization associations. Deemon tried all sorts of ways to stop this trip such as not having the company pay their annual membership.

10.18.16 The personal attack and retaliation against me from Deemon Monstah has allowed him to tamper with my vacation balance and payroll. The Company allows this type of discrimination, harassment and abuse.

Further Personal Abuses

03.10.16 I am continually denied of access to Seminary Online Program along with additional computerized charges to cell phone.
03.15.16 My home computer and printer still being tampered with causing delays in my ministerial assignments. Simple commands cannot be performed.

Threats

12.16.15 I am receiving threats of fire at church and home.

01.21.16 I have received an increase in the number of mailings for life insurance (I view this as a threat to my life) and loans. I have been to the company police, the township police and filed reports. I have been to the town District Attorney's office, the sheriff's office and filed a complaint. It is my hopes that should something happen to me that it will be noted in this record of vicious attacks. I realize this is an uphill battle with The Company police having a state-wide Memorandum of Understanding (MOU) which gives the Police jurisdiction with other police units.

01.28.16 My family and I are continuing suffering at the hands of abusive technical power of having messages sent to my phone that my daughter or granddaughter have dialed 911 when they have not. This is to threaten and scare me in not letting the world know what these criminals are doing.

03.15.16 I am being terrorized with police and guns images aimed at me and continually being shown on my home computer threatening messages.

04.07.16 The tentative court date is scheduled for May 2, 2016 and the purpose of this heighten abuse is to continue to terrorize and intimidate me and my family not to pursue this social injustice that Deemon Monstah, Holden Mitch, Jill Transzell, Stan W. Scramberg and team has been allowed to get away with because of their company positions.

04.07.16 I have received several threats pertaining to my income tax and being audited. Is that funny they are comingling the company and federal funds and yet they plan to audit my taxes. With their technology they have already taken my daughter's income tax return which will be added to the list for investigation. Who is auditing their income taxes? As I previously mentioned the select few steals money from my family and me and then uses to fund their war against me.

04.26.16 Normally, when I receive a threat it is a warning of what Deemon will do. Initially with these threats I was panicking and pondering on how to handle the upcoming situation. I now know that was part of the psychological torture. I now anticipate the threats so when he threatens me I can know how to direct the situation. My daughter's car is a 2006 so he threatens her vehicle all the time. The latest threat is that my daughter's car will be towed and ticketed by The Company Police. The select few have connections in Rahway. When my daughter goes to pick up my sister from work they plan to tamper with GPS signal to delay her traveling. The select few already used an old photo from an EZ PASS and placed it at a traffic light. Again, to have my daughter pay a fine and add points to her license. My daughter is an excellent driver and because of the hatred of me they have had her license suspended several times for no reason keeping her from driving to work and causing a hardship. I can only imagine the points that are on her license. After the federal investigation, I hope to have that all cleared for my daughter.

05.09.16 Threaten to stop granddaughter from attending kindergarten in the fall by delaying paperwork electronically. Threatening to have one granddaughter be retained because of technology in removing documents in book bag and hiding work assignments.

05.09.16 I am still being threatened with Identity Theft and sharing my information via the illegal federal technology given for Homeland Security. The Company police are now threatening to link false information to press about me because their personal lives and habits will be exposed along with the money laundering through Little Rock Consulting Firm.

I receive threats that the police plan to use the University Medical Research biological warfare on granddaughter to sleep walk. When are you going to investigate the ties between the

University Medical Research technology and their illegal medical testing?

05.12.16 I was informed of another threat that I will be in a car collision. I take this as another terroristic threat. Will someone view the Father Documents signed by Deemon Monstah and the technology brought by company police with federal funds!

06.24.16 Threaten to be audited by IRS and Income tax held. I am mindful that this company is connected to DMV, Post Office and the IRS. In addition, the anti-terrorism team has security access to all records. If I get audited, then I am telling the truth.

08.04.16 The threats still continue about taking life or doing bodily harm to me. Now the threat of stealing my Humanitarian Award for my religious and community service and academic accomplishments along with my other awards and achievements. I receive the cell phone, that my company ID and wallet will be taken every day.

08.05.16 The persistence of threats has now generated into the social silence of blocking out my cell phone. This type of repression has been done in the past. With the approval to listen in on cell phone calls and block communication, they have used it to block out my cell phone for huge blocks of time. With Sunday, being Communion Sunday and I use my phone to call and coordinate for Sunday Worship this will be an inconvenience for those trying to reach their Pastor. While there is nothing that can be done about the coincidence of construction, heavy traffic, delays and detours that is scheduled on Sundays being able to exercise one's First Amendment Right Freedom of Speech to place a call should be protected.

08.05.16 As the threats are intended to cause a terror and psychological abuse, I cannot dismiss the notion of what these federal criminals may do. Therefore, I will note the threat that was given to me of hitting and or stealing my car. It is noted that because I am grounded and rooted in my faith and as an American citizen, I will not submit to these domestic terrorists abusing the trust that was given them with the uniform. In addition, I thank Heaven for having a Bachelor's and Master's Degree in Public Administration and studied disaster preparedness along with a Master's in Divinity and Doctoral degree with studies in Pastoral Care and Counseling as well as being a Pastor surrounded by a strong foundation and network of Christian believing Pastors of the same. I say all of this not because of the hitting and stealing of my care but because of the threats of losing my life, my daughter and grandchildren's lives that are constantly made. These select few have placed dead animals in the street as warnings.

In addition, they are still tampering with the US Postal Mail which is a federal offense. I am still receiving countless offer for death benefits from various insurances along with medical insurance options for retirees.

09.07.16 In the attempts to continue his personal vendetta against me and my family and his unwanted inappropriate behavior, I was threatened with having my daughter and me being stopped for a supposedly tail light being out. As Pastor of a church, I have an important meeting at 7 pm with city officials today. My daughter simultaneously has to be a work. The threat is to use their influence as a police officer to have their colleagues have both of me my daughter stopped unnecessarily to have us late. (Wyner Punster is known for making phone calls to other police officers.)

09.19.16 I just received threat of blackout at my home tonight. I responded please bring the News Reporters and we can turn the lights on everything and everyone
10.25.16 Deemon Monstah has been allowed to continue his various terroristic acts. The latest threat is flooding my home with water. It took Deemon awhile but in July 2017, I returned home and my home was flooded.

12.27.16 The crimes have not stopped. The parsonage which is owed by the Bethel AME Church in which I am a pastor has been broken into and items stolen such as an antique secretary desk, and a cleaner machine. In addition, something was placed in the stove as a threat. Is anyone doing background checks on these people? Being arrested for lewd behavior and the circumstance surrounding that arrest? Not passing the bar exam, and lying on his resume to name a few. All have bearing on this case. I was sent to EAP because company police failed to do a proper investigation and follow up with me. Surely, he can be sent to EAP given his pathological lying, half-truths, and falsifying documents. There are signs of schizophrenia and depression. Every time I succeed in life outside of company, the domestic terrorism is elevated. Currently, I am successfully building a chapter for a National Women organization and now the parsonage has been broken into and items stolen. I have been specific in naming the culprits involved. The question is why is The Company allowing this to continue?

01.23.17 I received the normal junk mail with death benefits for insurance policies that they send to me. The illegal electronic acts of tampering with my bills are still continuing. The new tactic in terms of harassing is the attack of the senior citizens at my church with technical bullying. Because I expose them with the illegal use of the Hawk technology they used a similar technique with a bird. As with a dog sending signals they used a bird to be in the church and would not leave even with the doors and windows opened. The bird was programmed to intentional fly around during the opening of my sermon. This also shows the childishness of the culprits as well. In addition, the church window was broken, and I believe it was done to cause an economic hardship on the congregation which is comprised of mostly seniors ages 80 and over. With a broken window and the heat money is literally going out the window. Although the hole in the window is stuffed. How long will company allow the harassment and abuse of federal funds continue. They attack babies, children, females and they attack seniors. Why? Because we are Black and they can.

This sick demented racial abuse is being carried up until today 01.20.17. They are still tampering electronically with bills. The latest is the ADT bill from a former church I pastored which has been closed since June 2016 and all bills were paid.

As the terroristic games continues so does the abuse of technology with my employee time and my clocking in on Thursday, Jan. 12, 2017 at work.

01.27.17 Despite the great difficulty suffering through this agonizing racial discrimination and excruciating abuse, I still manage to lead a productive life and make a positive contribution to society while undergoing threats, phone being black out, emails deleted and no access to my home personal computer or printer. The latest threat is to cause a member of my national organization Executive Team to have a flat tire or car trouble. The State and The Company know who the select few are and I deemed those that do nothing as <u>accomplices</u> at this point. One cannot deny the fact that they did not know that a selected few is abusing Homeland Security procedures, policies and funds for their own racial discrimination. The conspiracies are done doing company time and using company resources with company approvals.

In addition, the Statewide Police MOU is a vehicle to ask other fellow racist officers to assist in the discriminating behavior such as racial profiling. This is no more than the Klu Klux Klan with uniforms and white shirts instead of white sheets. Instead of burning crosses, they tamper with your finances illegally and do other things that cause damage and money like flat tires. Most cars are electronically run, once they know the make and model of the vehicle they can send codes to cause things to appear to be wrong when in fact it is not.

Hopefully in keeping note of this someone will be man or woman enough to report this abuse to Washington, DC. We need a Federal Prosecutor to come in and handle this matter. I have tried twice to visit the Justice Department in Washington, DC. But because my car and cell phone are being tracked Capt. Linden Weeks made contact with the police at the door to not allow me in on both occasions.

I have been to the Governor's Office again which was a waste as the two aides Fetter sent down never followed up with me which confirms the Governor's involvement.

One of the on-going threats is the EAP and psychological evaluation. Why would I have a psychological evaluation done knowing that the doctor is related to University Research Medical Team? This is the same team that works on the biological warfare and cognitive behavior illegal testing on African Americans. I have had four psychological evaluations and I am fine. How many psychological evaluations are needed before something is done? I suggest that Deemon Monstah be tested. I believe this is a fear for both the company and Deemon Monstah as the truth will be revealed in his test. Why is Deemon Monstah fixated on my life and me? Outside of the fact, that I am an African American woman standing up to him.

The same terroristic tactics being used: Miscommunication with emails and phone calls, tampering with finances such as Prudential Insurance, church fuel bill, 401 K, and both church and personal bills to cause unnecessary financial hardships such as breaking the church window so the heat will escape through window now with a small church it is a financial hardship to replace window and the energy bill is increasing. In addition what was brought to Township Board of Education in the past and I will revisit it again is Deemon's illegal tampering with my grandchildren's school records. Everything is done electronically, grades, homework, teacher appointments, emails to and from teachers, and library books checkout.

01.31.17 I am still receiving threats of property damage being done to my home, my vehicle, the church and the church parsonage. In addition, to any lawsuit I may have please be advised the State and The Company will receive a separate lawsuit from the church if any more damage is done. So far, a window has been broken at the church along with threats of feces droppings. And the threat of mice placed at the parsonage. This is biological warfare against elderly African American seniors. The church and parsonage are used by the public primarily seniors over the age of 80 years old. If the exterminator comes and finds either feces or mice, I am forwarding the findings to church headquarters to begin legal action.

02.07.17 As the threats continue, using the same KKK tactics, I will continue to list them in the hopes that they do not occur.
1. My home being burnt down.
2. The roof of my house being tampered damages
3. The most recent threat is being inoculated with some type of drug. Having a stranger walk up to me and stick me to cause me to pass out and be sent to the hospital. Courtesy of University Research Medical Team doctors that supposedly took an oath to save people's lives sold their souls for money and conscious under the guise of science. What happen to medical consent? Black Lives does matter. So, the Tuskegee Experiments continue this time via technology. Review the technology contracts and approvals.

One person has already died because of Deemon Monstah's conspiracy. How more lives will have to be lost before something is done. Someone should step up to the plate and call the Justice Department. My phone email/texts are blocked. My laptop which this is the third one is destroyed. My mail is tampered with as well. I have tried countless times to reach out to Washington but with Mitch Holden as Chief of IS and Capt. Linden Weeks still using his connections from when he was an Inspector have made the task difficult if not impossible. Please note as long as I have breathe in my body I will continue to tell the truth and stand for Justice even with the death threat now placed on my life.

The latest threat being the use of biological warfare from the University Research Team.

04.04.17 I am not sure why I keep receiving threats of breaking into my home. I filed a police report when they broke in my home and stole my documents and jewelry. There is no reason for them to keep threating me about entering my home or threatening about medical testing. I am being coerced to try to force me to sign medical testing and to have entry into my home. It is not happening. I am not signing any stupid nonsense.

04.03.17 Being that technology involves engineering, the Technology University, Medical Research University and cell towers, stations with joint agreements and MOU's throughout the state this should be noted.

06.22.17 The Terrorizing started early this morning. I clocked in at 7:11 am. Let's see whether there is an issue with my time. On numerous occasions when I clocked, Deemon calls his self "mad" he blocks out my clocking in electronically as if I did not clock in. In addition, they continuously have my work ID pass not to activate at the entrance downstairs. All childish and stupid antics. Other threats are burning my house and shooting me.

Sexual Innuendos

In fact, it is with great urgency that Deemon Monstah receives counseling for his issues that he seems to want to draw me in to be a part of on a daily basis. Deemon believes that he is god. In addition to this delusion of being god, is the multi personalities that he acts out his frustration through one being his father who passed away. Deemon has unresolved issues with his father and the other personality is his feminine side named Jennifer.

Deemon is under the delusion and believes that he should have complete control of my life and I am nothing but mere property to him. Deemon has a great need to feel superior to me and so he continues to steal anything that acknowledges who I am such as my degrees, jewelry, money and awards. Currently, the following degrees are missing my degree for ordained ministry as deacon, my Master of Divinity Degree and my Doctor of Ministry. My degrees were on my computer both home, at work, and in addition on my cell phone. Deemon has electronically stolen my degrees because he did not want to be reminded of my accomplishments. If you notice and track the so-call work requests, you will see the <u>Pattern of Behavior</u>. Whenever I have an accomplishment, The Company receives a similar work request to do the same. Whenever I attend a function, the requestor's name or location is similar to what I am doing or have done. How long will the company be an Enabler to Deemon? How long do you think you can hide the Truth? As you can see, more and more Truth is revealed every day.

    I keep receiving information from them stating this is complicated. The fact of the matter is it is not complicated at all. We have people who have committed crimes. They need to be reported. It is just that simple. As it stands now, all the criminals manage to do is include more people as accomplices and jeopardize the company. Just because this involves the former Governor still does not make it complicated. Gov. Fetter has a known record within the state about his past illegal practices. This crime fits in and will answer a lot of the questions to other crimes that have been committed. The TRUTH will be told. I have two goals one is to be free from these psychos and the other is stop this from happening to others.

12.17.15 At or about 6:30 pm a crazy looking white man came to my door and tried to come in to my house. He stated he needed to come in and correct a bill. I threaten to call the Police. I believe that this was a terroristic threat due to my lawsuit and given to me as a warning.

12.17.15 At or about 2:35 pm at the request of Deemon Monstah and the company police just forward obscene photos and song to my personal cell phone. Lily heard the loud noise on my cell phone as I walked by to try to lower the volume.

12.21.15 At or about 10:43 am at request of Deemon Monstah, the company police just forward obscene photos and song to my personal cell phone.

02.01.16 I am continuing receiving photos of two half dress white males hugging with sexual lyrics playing with U2 Songs of Innocence written underneath. I have no idea of its purpose being sent to me.

02.01.16 I am continuously finding dead animals near my home. With the use of cognitive technology my grandson in staying home from school due to the false signals being sent to him of not feeling well or not hearing the alarm.

03.01.16 The psychotic behavior of the terrorizing team with their technology is becoming so abusive that they have elevated to writing curse words.

07.22.16 The sexual harassment continues via emails/texts/photos/advertisements and sexual threats to me and reference my 12-year-old granddaughter. This is child molesting. Capt. Weeks interrupts telephone/texts to granddaughter.

07.29.16 During the thorough investigation concerning the so-called film/event requests as you will see "unwanted messages".

09.07.16 In the attempts to continue his personal vendetta against me and my family and his unwanted inappropriate behavior, I was threatened with having my daughter and me being stopped for a supposedly tail light being out. As Pastor of a church, I have an important meeting at 7 pm with city officials today. My daughter simultaneously has to be a work. The threat is to use their influence as a police officer to have their colleagues have both of me my daughter stopped unnecessarily to have us late. Officer Wyner Punster is known for making phone calls to other police officers.

Furthermore, I am receiving more messages pertaining to being topless and reference to my bottom. It is not enough that I have to endure threats; I have to endure sexual threats as well.
Gov. Fetter, the State Chief of Homeland Security and the Transportation Commissioner were all notified of the illegal tampering via technology. All are a part of the racial discrimination via technology. This is racial domestic terrorism. In addition to my personal cell phone, personal lap top being blacked out. They have allowed Deemon Monstah to black out my work telephone. As I was receiving unwanted and inappropriate emails, videos and commercials on them. This is <u>Racial Cyber Bullying</u>. In addition, when I went to have the work cell phone replaced I was given a form to fill out and sign. I cannot be accountable for the illegal and inappropriate items they have place on this work phone. Deemon Monstah has a personal vendetta against me and he will stop at nothing to continue to harass me. I am not quitting my job. I am telling the truth. Again, I emphasize the <u>US Justice Department</u> should come in and do a clean sweep of all the racism, discrimination, abuse and retaliation that is going in the State under Governor Fetter. They should start at the top with Governor Fetter. Follow the illegal business deals, the bank accounts, and the dummy companies. How is he Governor of the State and not know about what is going on at The Company unless he is a part of it.

10.18.16 You will find all the evidence you need in Deemon Monstah's closet.

02.10.17 I was forwarded an email at the bottom of my screen stating, *"you are being watched".* What else is new? That is what he does. Gemini strikes again. I noted the time at 10:35 am (Intimidation 101 - Threat w/o follow up) If he is bold enough to do this here at the company, what makes the State think he is not doing this illegally at my home. If someone is keeping record, please note crime is not limited to on the property of the company.

04.17.17 My cell phone is still blacked due to the illegal use of the Homeland Security. The phone came on for a few minutes last night only to prompt me to respond to an unsolicited message. Still receiving requests to meet. I am firm and adamant about only meeting in the company conference room with witnesses. These creatures are ruthless, lying, crooked cowards using Homeland Security and Federal funds to discriminate against African Americans. The threats concerning my grandchildren's health, education and lives continues as I fight in this racial struggle with evil racists under Gov. Fetter's rule. Meanwhile, I unfortunately, have to endure the lewd comments coming from a person who has a fetish viewing child pornography and a crossdresser. The Board of Education will be notified pertaining to the education and grades of my grandchildren.

04.17.17 As usual Governor Fetter is still using Deemon Monstah's *feminine* side weakness as his flunky to lash out against me. The Empire or KKK spearheaded by the Governor Fetter is using the "Paranoid Projects" for the threat to coincide with my women's ministry luncheon. This is the flexing of power as it is just a matter of telephone call to an agency to make the request to the company via Community Relations. There is no real danger of my food on that date, but this is type of evil vindictive mind games Deemon Monstah likes to play.

05.05.17 The Cyber attacks has taken on a new demented twist with the unwelcome sexual advances, comments and encrypted messages which still are all part of the domestic terrorism being used. Some of the comments mentioned how they have devices to have holograms and appear in my bedroom, that they have technology that can see me dressing, how they can make me have nightmares, and threats of coming through my window and or roof of my house to do illegal things. In addition to those things, I also receive threats of stealing my laptop.

At the workplace, I have now started to walk the long way around to my cubicle to avoid walking by Deemon Monstah's office. To enforce the promise of these threats, Deemon now enters more frequently into Doug Wright's cubicle for supposedly work-related items or walks over when he knows Doug Wright is not at his cubicle. Also, Deemon now stands outside the cubicle and just waits since I now walk a different way. On Wednesday, May 3, he had his office light off when I entered through the double glass doors, so I thought he was out when I walked by the cubicle he walked out of the office next to his office. Deemon was in other office in the dark as if he was waiting for me to return as it is noticeable that I do not walk by Deemon Monstah's office when he is in since I start receiving the sexual threats.

05.05.17 After sending the email pertaining to the unwanted sexual advances, I am now receiving death threats.

05.12.17 Deemon Monstah was arrested years ago for lewd behavior which is public knowledge. Is this type of behavior resurfacing? I received a work request email asking about performing multiple acts. As you know the select few can send an email and make it seem as if came from anywhere USA. I have sent an email on Friday, May 12, 2017 at 9:59 am to bring clarity to this "multiple acts" request. In conjunction with the encrypted emails that are untraceable through my cell phone, I start to receive so-called work-related requests out of the normal language for such business requests.

05.22.17 Deemon also was making anonymous calls to Rev. Dr. Strong Kind about threats of child pornography being placed on his personal email. Fortunately, Dr. Kind filed a police complaint reporting the incident.

11.21.17 Tampering with my cable for my television and sent a new cable box to my home for cable and I did not ask for a new box. I now receive notices to hook up that box which I shall not.

I have listed several incidences, situations and occurrences in the hopes of showing how powerful this technology can be in the wrong hands. I survived to share my testimony. I received no justice. I hope in sharing my story justice prevails for others.

Invasion of Privacy

As I share this painful and tragic experience it is obvious that my human and civil rights have been violated. My Fourth Amendment rights were stripped away as I have not been able to be secure within my own person, house, papers or effect both at home and at work. My Eighth Amendment Right snatched away as I do not have "Equal Protection of the Law" as it is the supposedly law enforcers breaking the law who is depriving me. In addition, I am made to suffer cruel and unusual punishment as I am no more than a human science project and they hid behind their mask as they execute judgement on my life because I demanded my rights for equal pay for employment. My Fourteen Amendment was stolen when they broke into my home and I have been deprived of life, liberty and property. This is a Hate Crime plain and simple.

Chapter 5

Economic Injustice

We can have democracy in this country, or we can have great wealth concentrated in the hands of a few, but we can't have both.
Louis Brandeis[iv]

    There are great disparities positions, titles and pay at The Company. I recognize that racism is a major factor in Economic Injustice. In addition, Economic Injustice with the continued illegal use of Homeland Security access to utility companies. The PSE&G has tripled. The Union Township bill has quadruple. My sewer bill held. My daughter's PSEG Bill is astronomical. This is Harvey Fetter at his best attacking African American women and children.

01.13.16 illegally stealing money from my 401 K and my Wells Fargo Roth Account.

01.15.16 Electronically the select few are tampering with Church Tax information and payment $500 for October payment.

03.09.16 Since all bills are computerized I am being given additional charges on all bills and mail for credit accounts are delayed. This tampering with the US Postal Service and illegal computer tampering with accounts.

The question is who authorized this terroristic act with the selected few the Company Police and Holden Mitch.

03.07.16 I have received false telephone calls claiming to be a part of the Government Student Forgiveness Program. The purpose is to continue the economic injustice and financial hardship.

03.07.16 By making the false accusation back in 2011 of saying that I am a terrorist the company police have taken illegal access to both my personal finances and that of the church where I am the pastor. Deemon Monstah had Holden Mitch and Inspector Poe Ledesham identify me as a terrorist. With this false information, I was place under surveillance. Ask Deemon Monstah did he make that false statement that I was a terrorist when in fact he and the select few are the domestic terrorists. This should be a federal crime.

All of the church's bills that I pastored were paid. This included for water, sewer and taxes were all paid off with a zero balance as February 23, 2016. However, because of their illegal computer access I am sent bills dated February 26 with balances of $56.59 and $419.44 for sewer. The check from Seminary University for $2,020 was stolen. My ADT bill is quarterly of $135 they now have it coming monthly. They have generated a fake bill from Stanley Security for the church of $1,141.88 dated from 2013. The purpose of the financial harassment is to continue to threaten me and to keep me in financial ruins. Please note I plan to expose every single destructive act that comes to my attention until I am granted an opportunity at the Justice Department to tell of this terrorism and abusive acts against African Americans.

In addition, they create unnecessary incidents to have me have to take off from work such as having to meet with some of the above to discuss the financial issues that they create via technology. I will continue to share all letters and other information in order to clear my name and that of family members.

03.18.16 Electronically Holding Student Loan Payment to make it late. It is due today.

05.13.16 The company police are tampering with my maintenance Worry Free PSE&G bill. I am receiving false bills, phone calls stating bills are due, and the plan is cancelled. When I call PSE&G they state the bill and plan is fine.

The company police have the technology to send phone calls from various numbers and have false 1-800 numbers claiming to be different creditors from accounts that have been closed. In addition, the select few keep generating Church PSE&G bills.

07.29.16 In addition to the harassment one of the major purposes of this terrorism is to cause financial hardship. All avenues lead to the finances to impact my money.

10.21.16 The misappropriation of company resources, Federal Funds and Homeland Security technology continues.

During a real terroristic threat they can shut down technology such as my laptop and cell phone. They can also shut down utilities such as water, electricity and sewer. In my case, they are doing the opposite having the water run, pipes clogged, and lights come on. The company police are doing this all to increase my utility bills and cause a financial hardship. Deemon Monstah has made it up in his mind I should not have anything, so he seeks to find means and ways to steal my money and the company allows it because of the connection for Harvey Fetter. This ranges from high utility bills to repairs in the home and vehicles. Such as my daughter's tire ripping apart causing her to be late for her job interview then on the next day having the other tire rip apart trying to cause my daughter not to pick up her Driving Certificate and her daughter from school. The cost is another $30 for another tire. The personal vendetta against is also against my family. As the Advertising Company intersected my parent's moving truck and stole items off of them. This is another Federal offense in which it was approved by Governor Fetter. In trying to file a claim, my mail was intersected from the US Post Office in Newark, and it was Deemon Monstah that responded to all my letters. My father had insurance for full reimbursement for lost items. My father paid the additional insurance to ensure his items were covered and Deemon Monstah stole the items and the money with the help of the company Police and the advertising company. He robbed the elderly because they were my parents.

Furthermore, my Roth account was tampered with again. A fee of $105 was charged and when the bank tried to remove it, I was placed on hold for over 30 minutes. In addition, the $25 a month transfer to this account was also stopped. I am unable to continue to have the money transfer electronically. I have to physically go into the bank to make deposits to this account.

- My credit report was stolen as I will find on it identity theft as Deemon was allowed to ruin my credit with fake charges, late fees, and place a lien on my property all via technology.

- Because of the relationship with former Governor Fetter, Deemon Monstah with the assistance of Holden Mitch and certain the company police officers are allowed to continually abuse the system. The company is held accountable and responsible for all acts that they allow Deemon Monstah to commit. The question today is how long and how deep in the company will they allow Deemon Monstah to drag them in this mess. It is known that Deemon Monstah is bipolar and suffer from depression along with other psychological issues (review his past and personally life) and yet the company continues to allow him to hold a position and make poor and dangerous decisions on behalf of The Company.

- The ultimate goal in this was for me to quit and to be broke. I refuse to do either.

Economic Abuse

The economic abuse is so prevalent and rampant that I have made sub categories of the economic abuse. Deemon Monstah's goal was to attack every area of my life economically because this is the god he worships. I see money as a means for transaction. Deemon sees money as a power weapon to take from the poor and needy and to keep them enslaved. Deemon believes that if he takes your money you cannot eat, have a place to sleep, clothes to wear and any other niceties of life. Deemon's goal was to make me destitute. Deemon attacked anyone that showed me kindness or assisted me in some way. He retaliated by tampering illegally with their finances. If he could not tamper with their finances he hit their car, or through Harvey Fetter's connections had them fired or removed. The ultimate goal was always an economic frontal attack.

Work Related Economic Abuse

09.14.16 There is no new strategy on this abuse of position and power. They are still electronically tampering with my bills and banking transactions. They have tapped into the PSE& G & the Water bill to increase it.

10.03.16 I have submitted numerous requests for a new computer and in addition to several tickets to the help desk on tasks because of the computer malfunction and Deemon Monstah's access to my emails.

o   I am now required to finish of the Dallas trip which was submitted months ago. The initial delays were lack of signatures through the system, then whose financial responsibility of paying for July trip. Now, I am still having great difficulty with the system and accessing it. Furthermore, my expense report was given back after I obtained signatures as they do not use paper anymore. I have explained because of the tampering with my computer I am unable to process and type of financial document. The purpose of these intentional delays is to not give me my reimbursement. This is just another form of discriminating harassment. My coworkers go on trips all the time and never have any problems. I on the other hand cannot process and simple reimbursement for an organization that company is supposedly supporting. The Minority Professional Organization's mission statement is to level the playing field. How can the company level the playing field if they do not allow you on the field? As it stands now, I am owed a reimbursement from the Dallas trip and $125 for my Minority Professional Organization membership.

10.11.16 The economic injustice continues as I have an antiquated computer that will not allow me to upload the receipts for the expense report. This is Deemon Monstah's way of stopping my reimbursement from the Dallas trip and the Minority Professional Organization membership. Again, continuous abuse of the technology with Mitch Holden and the Governor Harvey Fetter's approval.

10.04.16 The discrimination and harassment continues with the computer malfunction and me not being able to have the necessary equipment as my coworkers. This abuse is also costing me money as I am not allowed to put in for my reimbursement for Minority Professional Organization Membership and the Dallas trip. My payment to Minority Professional Organization on May 3, 2016 was stolen and never made it to Minority Professional Organization National. Because I have the money order and did a returned received which proves the US Postal mail was tampered with by a select few Company Police at the request of Deemon Monstah. They are still playing games. Deemon who has access to my computer given to him by Mitch Holden tampered with the invoice from 2015.

11.28.16 The terrorizing and discrimination continues as I am not allowed the same privileges as my white co-workers. Printer does not work and P: Drive for files are missing. I am not sure how I am expected to perform the tedious task that I have been given when I am not given adequate computer technology as my coworkers. Who supposedly suffers more in this harassment? Taxpayers for the waste of time and resources.

Personal Economic Abuse

o   02.25.16 Seminary computer access denied. I am unable to complete assignments
o   03.14.16 Using technology to illegal inflate Church PSE & G Bill
o   03.26.16 Because the terrorism and abuse are allowed to continue my home computer has shut down.
o   The attacks are now centered on my daughter and grandchildren
o   Illegal tampering with grandchildren's grades electronically
o   Phony items placed on credit report
o   Phony liens against my property
o   Sending phony medical bills with inflated fees
o   Continuing to tamper with creditors & bank balances
o   Illegally adding charges to car loan
o   Falsifying letters from Federal Student Loans on my daughter's account
o   Held and illegally tampering with US Post Office Mail
o   07.25.16 Still tampering with computer generated bills when payments are being received to cause late fees and increase interest.   All Financial Institutions computerized records have been tampered with such as Prudential life insurance. Increased amount of   loan.

08.04.16 The criminal activity has reached federal level in violations such tampering with   my Credit Report taken because it shows identity theft of other false accounts.

o   08.04.16 As another demonstration of the racial injustice, I am being penalized via   economic injustice. Since we live in a technical world my personal accounts are being   tampered with and inflated fees are being added to them. The demented logic is to have   me be charged these outrageous false fees to compensate for the amount of the trip   because his irrational logic is I am not equal to my coworkers and should not be allowed   to the same rights as them to travel and have an opportunity for growth and development. With the technology of diverting calls to a fake 1.800 number it is difficult to contact creditors to correct this federal financial fraud. So far, below are the additional fees charged above my normal accounts:

- Ashley Stewart $27.
- Verizon Wireless $50.91
- Water bill $26.59
- Express Scripts $10

- 09.14.16 There is no new strategy on this abuse of position and power. The select few are still electronically tampering with my bills and banking transactions. The select have tapped into the PSE& G & the water bill to increase it.
- 09.19.16 As it is known, the company Police has the technology to black out telephones as part of Homeland Security for protection on trains. The selected few is currently illegally using this technology and blacking out my personal cell phone. I have been to Verizon twice to have the telephone checked. It works temporarily while inside of Verizon. Once I leave the property it of course blacks out. The purpose of this is because the culprits are afraid that I will forward information to every one of the corrupt illegal abuse of technology and tax payers' money. I am not afraid of them nor am I am afraid of telling the truth especially this election year. The public should be made aware of what a selected few racists have the abusive power to do here in America. They are domestic terrorists and should be prosecuted to the fullest extent of the law these the company Police, no passing the bar lawyers and representatives of the company. I have been very direct in the listing of who they are and have been.

- 10.14.16 As the oppression of African Americans plight here at the company continues, the illegal use of technology in tampering with my vacation time and my daughter's pay check. As with all racism it has the economic injustice piece that works to also enslave and kept enslave. The blacking out of my personal cell phone and laptop as well as The Company cell

phone to keep me disconnected from an electronic world.
Understandably so, as I will inform the world of the injustices done here at the company will the blessing of the Governor Fetter at the helm.

o   10.13.16 As I endure the racial struggle here at THE COMPANY. The standard which has become their standard in still illegally tampering in the computers of my creditors. The PSE&G and meter reading has been tampered and holding my mail which is also a federal crime. Lead by our Governor Fetter to keep the Father Document and other illegal dealings quiet. All it takes is a simple thorough investigation. My cell phone and home computer still blacked out.

o   11.01.16 $15.00 fee has been on my mortgage bill since June 4, 2015 where my electronic payments had been stopped between the time of March 2015 to June 2015. There was a Property Inspection requested and done by Deemon Monstah who tried to buy my mortgage.

o   11.01.16 One would think that the narcissistic individual of Deemon Monstah would be stopped by now, but you allowed and even encourage this behavior by allowing it to continue.

o   12.01.16 As expected with the abuse of the racial profiling from a selected few the company Police at the request of Deemon Monstah and the approval of Gov. Harvey Fetter they were allowed to falsely stop my daughter in Virginia. As requested documents of her driving record and driving certificate of safe driving was forwarded to the Judge. Supposedly, the documents were not received while I have a post office certified mail receipt. A fee of $225 and the threat of my daughter losing her licenses have been issued.

o   Deemon Monstah with his hatred for me has let this cancerous infection spread to my daughter. Deemon is in a rage because it was my daughter who drove me to Texas for the

Minority Professional Organization Dallas trip. He his vendetta has now maliciously extended to my innocent daughter for assisting her mother. The goal here to cause unnecessary anguish, economic hardship to her and me as well as to stop her from driving. With four children and a full time-job is it imperative that she has her license.

o	Why does the company continue to allow such abuse and more importantly why does the Governor of the State?

o	12.02.16 As is the norm when I am traveling my cell phone gets blacked out. As a pastor and grandmother, I am unable to be accessible to my family and congregation as the racist illegal acts continue. The utility bills are still being tampered with. For the month of November, I received two water bills from Water. Symbolic of the illegal acts they are able to just wash away because of the ties with former Governor Fetter and the Homeland Security in Washington DC. It is no surprise that Governor Fetter used his position as Governor in the conspiracy with Homeland Security and that is why Deemon Monstah is allowed and encouraged to continue to use Federal Funds to support his racist behavior. There is no consequence or repercussion for this continued retaliatory psychotic behavior.

o	12.07.16 The hatred of me advancing in any area is still progressing with Deemon Monstah. Because he is allowed to abuse the Homeland Security and monitor my finances and my daughter's. Deemon is continuously causing hardships to cost me money. The economic injustice that this person has been allowed to do is unbelievable in a land supposedly of freedom. My daughter's tire was flattened this morning causing her to have to withdraw money from my account and pay an ATM withdrawal fee. While I budget to move ahead since I am being discriminated against by not being promoted or upgraded in this company. Deemon hates the idea of me having money and able to save while he causes unnecessary expenses for me and my family.

The illegal technology is still being used for the water bill and electric bill.

Please note you will see tires flattened a couple times because over the period of ten years this is what has been. You will also see the Dallas trip had a major impact on Deemon Monstah in several areas. First because he believes I am not entitled to the same educational opportunities as my coworkers. Secondly, Deemon Monstah had a major melt down because I had an opportunity to travel. Thirdly, my daughter was able to attend the trip with me and did all the driving this elevated his hatred of her and vowed to go after her because she drove me to see my son who I had seen in three years due to the financial constraints. The reuniting of the three of us along with his lovely wife made for a great family reunion. Furthermore, she was six months pregnant. We had a great time and this joyous occasion raised the hatred level to a new high. Deemon was going to make me pay for this. How dare I enjoy myself when he decided I would live in poverty and shame. Deemon has now declared war and will lead the charge on the frontal attacks on me economically.

Family Abuse

o   12.16.15 Deemon is allowed to tamper with the bus schedule again. This also impacts on-time performance. With all the trouble vehicle and financial trouble my daughter has been having she is taking public transportation. I cannot count how many times they have revoked my daughter's licenses. It cost $100 each time we have to get them reinstated.

o   12.16.15 Deemon Monstah via THE COMPANY Police has place cat feces in my daughter's apartment. It did this same thing in 2013 at my home.

o   12.18.15 Daughter's cell phone, flat screen TV, and mirror on car destroyed because of this illegal use.

o   02.09.16 Use of technology daughter's car and cell phone, keeping sending text about 911, took work cell phone again, chemical warfare with flu like symptoms, chemical warfare with drying out skin and hair. Electronically taped into IRS and stole daughter's income tax refund.

o   02.04.16 Used technology to jam home computer, printer and personal cell phone.

o   03.21.16 Used technology to inflate daughter's PSE&G bill

o   03.27.16 Used technology illegally to steal daughter's identification for work and $5 she had for the bus.

o   07.25.16 Tampered with daughter's social service programs for children via technology. Letters generated stating she was no longer receiving certain benefits.

o   10.26.16 Currently, my daughter's bank account has been frozen and work check is unable to be deposited and processed due to illegal tampering with technology along with bank fees related to the incident.

Ministry Abuse

o   12.16.15 THE COMPANY Police made two phony calls to me pretending to be the Marines for Toys for Tots and stating I had 100 toys and then followed up with a female calling stating they gave her my number to get toys. The number on the caller ID was the same number of the Marine's office I spoke to on the phone. When I went to pick up the toys it was the original amount of toys I selected for ten children. I inquired about the phone calls and of the soldier name I gave no one knew who that person was. Because I believed I was receiving 100 toys, I paid to have the storage room cleaned at church, a new lock placed on the door and the door refinished. Therefore, I spent money for the church unnecessarily.

o   12.16.15 Deemon Monstah had the church garbage not picked up
o   01.14.16 block call for Fire Extinguisher to be checked at church endangering the lives of congregation.
o   02.29.16 Tampered with computer for Church PSE&G Bill and doubled it $1,032. How long will the company allow this type of abuse with technology to continue? Cut Deemon Monstah's power source and all the technological crime with me will end. It is Deemon Monstah's hope that if he continues to tamper with my creditors, the church's finances and my daughter's financial documents that he will bully me into giving up.

o   03.21.16 Stole church money.
o   03.28.16 The abuse with the illegal use of technology is tampering with church documents. This is why we need the Justice Department in Washington DC since the company cannot resolve the issue with the company Police and the terrorism. I welcome the opportunity to speak at a congressional hearing about the abuse of federal tax dollars to support racism, discrimination, and internal terrorism within the company.

o   04.03.16 Vandalize & Stole television from Church.

o   07.25.16 The terrorism continues against Black Clergy and their families with the illegal use of Homeland Security to stop families by using other Police Officers similar to illegal act done in Passageville Patrol Police. Passageville falsified the electronic device to charge outrages fees, fines and trump up traffic charges.

o   09.29.16 This illegal use of technology is impacting my ministry greatly as I was unable to connect with members for our weekly Bible Study call in conference. Our tax dollars are paying for this discriminating abuse. A pastor cannot have Bible Study because a few racist people are abusing their positions and both

federal and state tax dollars. The sad part is Governor Fetter knows and approves.
o   10.28.16 The attack against African Americans and Black Clergy continues. The illegal use of technology from Homeland Security continues as my cell phone, lap top is still blacked out, and I am unable to fulfill my ministerial duties at my optimum level. This misuse of Federal Funding is impacting churches and nonprofit organizations specifically minorities, women and children. But because I am a person of color I guess it is okay to tampering with the following ministries I am involved in working:
o   Women's Ministry, Coordinator to promote women in ministry
o   To provide gifts for children of parents in prison
o   Coordinate with Marines to donate toys to children that are less fortunate
o   Domestic Violence Awareness – coordinate opportunities to share awareness and assist other non-profits
o   Nonprofit that provides information on building the family unit and provides meals while in session
o   Interfaith Ministerial Alliance – upcoming coordinator for Thanksgiving Service to enhance the Biblical teaching of diversity and love.
o   District Ministerial Alliance to coordinate Christmas party and gathering of Ministers and family for fellowship and updates of the districts.
o   National Women's Organization – that promote Women. I am unable to join online and share in the information that is provided and participate in assisting in their nonprofits initiatives.
o   Local School – to provide junior and high school students an opportunity to play their instruments and be a part of the local worship service.
o   We Keep Our Promises Initiative – the focus is to promote the youth and work with town for employment and training

02.01.18 This morning I walk outside, and my new car was started and running. I knew when I purchased the vehicle that in dealing with these racist cowards that this would be an issue. So as I suspected it was. To have me delayed coming to work my vehicle was started and I had to take time to shut it off and lock the doors. You see with the new technology they have mastered not only technology such as starting my vehicle which is no great feat, but they have learned how to break down matter. Meaning that any item they can breakdown the molecules in them in relocate them somewhere else. Just like water can be a liquid, steam or frozen as a solid. They can change the molecules and relocate items. They have not mastered the human flesh yet. So if you have the item touching your skin, they cannot transform it. All the proof needed is to review the agreements between University Medical Research and the Federal Government which they have allowed the company access to illegally.

As it stands now, the only thing that they can continue to do is attack me economically. The plan is that eventually I will fold if I have no resources. There is only one flaw with that plan. I am a servant of the Most High. I have heavenly blessings. I have survived over ten years of their abuse because I do not rely on material wealth.

o   12.02.16 As is the norm when I am traveling my cell phone gets blacked out. As a pastor and grandmother I am unable to be accessible to my family and congregation as the racist illegal acts continue. The utility bills are still being tampered with enormous fees. For the month of November I received two water bills from the Water Company. Symbolic of the illegal acts they are able to just wash away because of the ties with Governor Fetter and the Homeland Security in Washington DC. It is no surprise that Governor Fetter used his position as Governor in the conspiracy with Homeland Security and that is why Deemon Monstah is allowed and encouraged to continue to use Federal Funds to support his racist behavior. There is no consequence or repercussion for this continued retaliatory psychotic behavior.

o   12.01.16 As expected with the abuse of the racial profiling from a selected few company police officers at the request of

Deemon Monstah and the approval of Gov. Harvey Fetter they were allowed to falsely stop my daughter in Virginia. As requested documents of her driving record and driving certificate of safe driving was forwarded to the Judge. Supposedly, the documents were not received while I have a post office certified mail receipt. A fee of $225 and the threat of my daughter losing her licenses have been issued.

o   Deemon Monstah with his hatred for me has let this cancerous infection spread to my daughter. Deemon is in a rage because it was my daughter who drove me to Dallas. His vendetta has now maliciously extended to my innocent daughter for assisting her mother. The goal here to cause unnecessary anguish, economic hardship to her and me as well as to stop her from driving. With four children and a full time-job is it imperative that she has her license. Why does COMPANY continue to allow such abuse and more importantly why does the Governor of the State? The trip happened in 2016 and we are still dealing with false fees and fines being sent. I hope the Governor of Virginia look into this matter. Did the company police call the state of Virginia and arrange for my daughter to be stopped?

o   11.28.16 The terrorizing and discrimination continues as I am not allowed the same privileges as my white co-workers. The printer does not work and P: Drive for files are missing. I am not sure how I am expected to perform the tedious task that I have been given when I am not given adequate computer technology as my coworkers. Who supposedly suffers more in this harassment? Taxpayers for the waste of time and resources.

01.31.18 The criminals are still playing the same economic game as they know the end is near. I purchased a new vehicle and I wanted the old vehicle towed. Because they have access to abuse the 1.800 numbers when I call my car insurance I keep getting one of the company police. The officers even use their names. They are refusing to allow me to contact my insurance company so I may have the 2006 vehicle towed. As the vehicle is costing me money daily to be insured when I can have it towed. Again, another example of Economic Abuse this is supposed to have me pressured to do whatever they say. I shall not.

8.24.17 As much as I try to escape the evil clutches of Deemon Monstah the more he tries to hold me in his deceitful wicked tactics. His latest illegal act under the authority of former Governor Fetter and the assistance of Holden Mitch and Officer Linden Weeke is tampering with my bank account. In Deemon's demented mind, he wants to show me that I need to sign his illegal unethical deal with him in which I shall not make any deals with the devil. They have taken $21.99 out of one of my accounts so that it will have a zero balance. The purpose is that Deemon wants to emphasize that I have nothing without him. While he is sadly mistaken and terribly misguided, it is the opposite. The sooner the company and the state get rid of Deemon Monstah the better the world will be. Deemon has done nothing since he has been here but undermine, lie and steal from the company and the state. If you check the record since 2008, Deemon has been nothing but trouble since he walked through the door. Human resources should look at the number of people who retired early and number people who quit both black and white. If ever there is bad news Deemon Monstah is it. Keep Deemon Monstah and you keep trouble. Deemon is a drama queen. He thrives off of keeping trouble brewing. Unfortunately, this is who and what he is. He does not know any better. The best thing for him as this point is to be locked up and put away for life. He is a detriment to others, the organization, the state and society in general. Deemon Monstah cares about no one and nothing. The company and the state will have to give an account of the heinous acts Deemon has done and they did nothing to stop him. The crimes Deemon has committed will be on their hands. I look forward to the day this is in the news for the world to know the Truth. Corporate Policy states it has a Zero Tolerance while Deemon tries to empty my account to a Zero Balance.

Cruel and Heartless

05.04.17 As the technological tactics continues I have an email from a requestor dated May 3, 2017 at 9:37 am. As the company police have the technology to send an email from anywhere and invade your synapse gap train of thought the attached email is a sad attempt to start the discredit approach. Please note the decisions made were after Patricia Tressa called and stated she spoke to Deemon Monstah. I in turn forwarded as my supervisor instructed based on her direction from Deemon. This is the type manipulation that goes on every day with him. Deemon manipulates situations to try to set me up all the time. This is not the first sad attempt, nor will it be the last. The Governor allows Deemon to continue knowing he has a DNA flaw and mental issues.

05.02.17 With Deemon Monstah's <u>Obsessive Compulsive Disorder</u> and hatred against me, my family and associates his vicious attacks that Governor Fetter allows is still continuing with the blacking out of my cell phone, deleting my personal emails and tampering with both the church and my personal bank account. The question is "How long Governor Fetter will people of color people suffer at the hands of this Statewide Structural Racism?" It is bad enough with the economic injustice of the company and the changing over to the <u>Grade</u> system similar to what the cell towers use with the basic signal within neurons and the <u>Action Potential</u> which is a rapid shift in the electrical charges across the cell membrane of neurons so as people of color walk through station terminals you can tap into their <u>Synapse Gap</u>.

05.19.17 History has a way of repeating itself. Since the past terrorizing tactics did not work and they have no other weapons to attack me they have resorted to the old tactics. The list so far is as follows:

- Still stealing money via technology out of my checking account.

- Still delaying my daughter paperwork via technology in her new position to cost me more money via checking account
- Still delaying the company buses and putting other customers and commuters in that delay as well. Today's bus was 7 minutes late.
- Still using unethical maneuvers within his position as Senior Director such as not paying the Minority Professional Organization Membership.
- Still using the Governor's Crossover Tunnel tactic of causing traffic delays when I need to attend meetings. I hope no ambulance needs to get through.
- Still have the ultimate goal of having me overworked and underpaid. He wants to find ways and means to drain me both physically, mentally and most of all financially. Unfortunately, outside of his authorization and approval for Governor Fetter, of harassment this will not happen. I know who they are want they are doing. Once the Federal Prosecutor steps in and investigate this will be over. I have a proven track record of success and will continue to maintain my status. I am determined to not allow racism, envy, and domestic terrorism interfere with my destiny.
- Still using technology to send fraudulent requests to waste company time and resources. For every fake request I receive I have to send internally for review. That is not fair to the other internal stakeholder team to have to waste time on a frivolous request of a demented person who wants to control my time. Not to mention the paper and the emails. But the Governor feels it is time and tax dollars well spent.

05.17.17 With the ongoing threat of the week ramming my vehicle, tampering with income, threats of IRS audit, identity theft and stealing/falsifying of my home documents at the Elizabeth Court I am dealing with the racial profiling of police. I was stopped by a white police office for no reason when leaving the NAACP meeting and told this was a warning for me! In lieu of the all the illegal things a select few racist police officers are doing within the company police force you would think they would stop by now. In the past Captain Wyner Punster was the one making the calls to other police officers to harass my family and friends. Now it is Capt. Linden Weeke who is handling the matters personally. What is the Police Chief doing at the company? Is he only a figure head and the Klan are allowed to run the Police Force? No investigations, no follow up, no reports and therefore no prosecution of the abuse as it continues to run rampart. While I was issued a warning last night, I will continue at full steam ahead in the pursuit of justice and my civil rights. No racist police officer, racial structure, or Klansman will stop me from pursuing my freedom. I have a right to be here! I have a right to speak up! I have a right to advance! As quiet as it is kept or, so they think they are enlisting more Klansmen via the company police force. Someone needs to review the police demographics and check their psychological records. Racial Bias awareness training is not enough. Anyone can place the correct answer on a sheet of paper, but what happen when the select few are still making racist decisions with people's lives. With racists' police officers and the illegal use of medical research and technology the state is in grave danger. They are setting the camp for Genocide via drugs, psychological disorders and arrests of minority. Check the arrest records and so-called charges!

05.15.17 The new threat is ramming my vehicle and breaking my legs.

Noted for record four helicopters were hovering over home this morning. People were asking did something happening as they did not see anything mentioned on the news around 6:00 am – 6:30am. This is our tax dollars in the air. Since I have barracked my home to stop the break-ins, I receive more threats.

06.29.17 The company has failed far below the scale by comparison and below its own standards concerning its African Americans employees in promotion and reclassification. The persistent tendency to overlook and permanently marginalize African Americans has become an entry to a much larger system of racial stigmatization. This so-called legalized discrimination and social exclusion lays the foundation to the racial caste system. Being permanently barred from opportunity and training. This prejudice is sadly a common routine and frequently occurs. The normal discrimination plan of action is to send employees to EAP for a psychological evaluation after they have filed an EEO Compliant. If that does not work the subversive tactic of the so-called "department reclassification" is done and the person who filed an EEO complaint position is abolished to force the employee to move to another department where the former racist supervisor has an associate who will do his racist deeds. The original racist culprit deletes a person's position to have them forcibly removed from the department then rename the position to hire someone new usually white, younger and with more pay. I am certain that after the release of this book to expect this treatment for telling the truth.

In fact, it is with great urgency that Deemon Monstah receives counseling for his issues that he seems to want to draw me in to be a part of on a daily basis. Deemon believes that he is god. In addition to this delusion of being god, is the multi personalities that he acts out his frustration through one being his father who passed away. Deemon has unresolved issues with his father and the other personality is his feminine side named Jennifer.

The plan now is to continue to manipulate my schedule, caused unnecessary confusion with documents I need to transact business such as my mortgage statement and diplomas, and to drain me financially with interest fees, late fees and all sorts of other electronic ways to steal money from me. Deemon holds my personal checks I write for weeks and or months in cyber space before releasing them to be deposit. Deemon also does the same for the church checks. He continuously adds unnecessary fees on bills for both my personal home and the church. Deemon holds bills and changes the billing dates. Deemon does all of these things to mess me up financially.

Deemon is under the delusion and believes that he should have complete control of my life and I am nothing but mere property to him. Deemon has a great need to feel superior to me and so he continues to steal anything that acknowledges who I am such as both my degrees. Currently, the following degrees are missing my degree for ordained ministry as deacon, my Master of Divinity Degree and my Doctor of Ministry. My degrees were on my computer both home, at work, and in addition on my cell phone. Deemon has electronically stolen my degrees because he did not want to be reminded of my accomplishments. If you notice and track the so-called email requests you will see the <u>Pattern of Behavior</u>. Whenever I have an accomplishment, the company receives a similar request for the same. Whenever I attend a function, the requestor's name or location is similar to what I am doing or have done. How long will the company be an enabler to this person? How long do you think you can hide the Truth? As you can see, more and more Truth is revealed every day.

I keep receiving information from them stating this matter is complicated. The fact of the matter is it is not complicated at all. We have people who have committed crimes. They need to be reported. It is just that simple. As it stands now, all the criminals manage to do is include more people as accomplices and jeopardize the company. Just because this involves the former Governor still does not make it complicated. Gov. Fetter has a known record within the state about his past practices. This crime fits in and will answer a lot of the questions to other crimes that have been committed. The TRUTH will be told.

The spinal cord is compared to a communication site. The protected inside of the bony vertebrae of the spine is an inch-thick gelatinous bundle of nerves fibers. This structure, called the spinal cord acts as the central communication conduit between the brain and the rest of the body. Millions of nerve fibers carry motor information from the brain to the muscles, while other fibers bring sensory information (such as touch, pain, and body position) from the body back to the brain.

Cabling is important! It is the frequency of action potentials that changes with the intensity of stimuli. Once your central nervous system receives information in the form of action potentials, it can process the information to formulate a response to it. The Central Nervous System (CNS) depends on the sensory neurons passing their signals to other neurons in the CNS. The Nervous System is just another cable transferring information.

07.11.17 Deemon Monstah is using technology again and was able to delay my regular scheduled bus on yesterday July 10, 2017 to stop in front of the Dollar Store. The plan as previously stated is to force me to sign an illegal unethical agreement for a phony position to work in another department. Please note, the department has been in several class action discrimination lawsuits and outside of the Police department leads the way for the racial discrimination at the company. Deemon wants me to report to one of his associates who have plans to harass me until I retire or quit. The so-called promotion is a low level phony manager's position that will rely on the computer in which they will have control of to start the write ups of poor workmanship and errors. I have declined on numerous times that I am not interested in any of their diabolical illegal and unethical scams.

08.01.17 The continued abuse with tampering with my GPS so I was unable to receive accurate directions to have me driving around until I stumbled upon the state Turnpike and have to pay. Who tracks the illegal usage of when they can use the Homeland Security equipment? In addition, to the ongoing death threats with the latest being running me off the road or having a car accident and since I reported the illegal use of the Hawk equipment in an EEO Complaint of retaliation in which no investigation has been done. The new threat is of giving me a flat tire so that I can be stranded all night as they can divert signals with the GPS and cell phone. This is another form of retaliation and terrorizing tactic to intimidate me.

If I cannot interest the federal government in helping others like me with the ongoing discrimination and retaliation, what about looking into the mass privatization and outsourcing that the company is doing along with bringing in more chiefs and high paying salaries. Follow the money. Employees that have been here for ten, fifteen and twenty years cannot get a raise, but yet you can bring someone into the company with no experience starting off at over $100,000 a year to do nothing.

08.14.17 Where is the Company's responsibility and accountability? The Company has hired people in the senior management positions without doing extensive background checks on them for psychological issues, identity issues, drug and alcohol, prior police records, their prior jobs or education. There are supervisors with these known disorders including lying on their resumes making decisions over the lives of people of color. Why is a bipolar, an alcoholic or a person who suffers from depression, a convicted felon arrested for lewd behavior, and who has lied about credentials allowed to make a recommendation to send another employee to EAP when they themselves have personal issues they have not dealt with compiled with the fact of them being a racist? Have you been following the patterns of disturbed behavior over the last ten years? There is some serious brain dysfunction, biochemical factors consideration due to abnormalities in brain functions and total disturbance of emotion and perception. It is known that schizophrenia tend to run in families and there are genetic factors that also play in the role. Combine that with a racist belief and tendencies along with identity issues and multi personality issues and you have a devastating psychological disorder individual running a department. How many people have left this department within the last ten years? How many EEO complaints must one receive before an eyebrow is raised about their behavior? The company has a corporate social responsibility.

10.06.17 I am still receiving the ongoing threat of having my daughter arrested by the County Sheriff's Office if I do not submit to Governor Harvey Fetter's illegal scheme.

As requested by Patricia I am taking the check requisition training. Let the record show this is by no means reflect that I plan to transfer to another Division. The division that Deemon wants to transfer me to has the most class action discrimination lawsuits outside of the Police Department. They are known for blatantly discriminating in that division. I would never transfer to work in that division for that very reason.

10.10.17 They are now reverting back 2013 with the other illegal medical tactics such legs cramps, and coughing. He is trying to make me take a sick day and stay home. I am perfectly healthy.

10.10.17 The latest threats are tampering with my father's medical records and medical tests which are computerized and starting an electrical fire in my attic. In addition, a fire warning for the company was given today as a test. With the additional threat of the hit and run with a vehicle. I cross at the crosswalk every day. Vehicles are supposed to stop when a pedestrian is in the crosswalk. The street light that is placed in the location of the crosswalk is not working. The local police have been notified numerous times in the past.

Furthermore, the ongoing tampering of my grandchildren's school records is still occurring. Today, my grandson was told he would have to sit in the auditorium all day for failure of having an immunization shot. There was neither notification given nor no policy again computer tampering with school records. My daughter's social security card information was taken out of her phone and my cell phone again, illegally technology tampering. In addition to Harvey Fetter's orders of causing havoc today, there is Deemon Monstah with the multiple personality disorder and today he is his father.

10.30.17 Harvey Fetter with his harassing of stopping of me from completing my expense report from July 2017 for reimbursement of $20 and my reimbursement of my Minority Professional Organization membership of $125. In addition, stooping as low as stealing money from children to cause me a financial hardship. The stealing of money from my granddaughter by using a physical change of matter. The attack is also continuous on the church where I pastor as well. I am now receiving documents pertaining to the tax exemption of the church.

11.03.17 The terroristic threats today are hitting my daughter and my car and or flattening the tires.

11.29.17 Domestic Terrorism has risen to a new level of threat. Harvey Fetter had three white men supposedly police officers' approach my daughter while she was taking her daughter to pre-K. They did not identify themselves as police officers nor did they show her a badge. They claimed they she looked like someone they were pursuing. The photo they showed my daughter was a dark-skinned woman and my daughter is a lighter hue. Three police cars pulled up and one police officer got out of the vehicle and approached my daughter. They pushed my daughter and were trying to separate her from her four-year daughter. This happened around 8am this morning. They made a four-year-old little girl stand against the fence while they surrounded her mother. A four-year-old has to now live with that trauma. There was a total of about seven white police officers surrounding an African American woman unarmed walking her daughter to school who is in pre-k. Please note the lawsuit will be amended to include this incident of police brutality and racial profiling. The purpose of this racial profile and police brutality was another feeble attempt to intimidate me to drop my civil case of violating my constitutional rights by assaulting my daughter.

12.04.17 Same old sick demented game, but with new names for the work requests. Harvey Fetter has Deemon Monstah with the help of Holden Mitch pulling old cell tower requests from the archives and has me to redo them over again. These will be new to Patricia, but as the abuse circle continues they just pull the same old request and change the location acquisition representative's name. Then after a few emails they change the name again for the same project in the subject line. In other words, Deemon does not have a job. He spends his day making up phony requests, reviewing my emails and trying to find ways to ask stupid questions to cause more unnecessary work and confusion. It is ashamed and so embarrassing for him.

There is no leadership for the department, no vision, no goals, no direction and no respect. Basically, Deemon comes in after 9am closer to 10am and at 3:45pm he leaves. As if we all can't see that he changed the time on the clock in office by 15 minutes. Get a life. By the way, he needs to stop coming over and bothering Doug Wright. He comes over with the stupidest questions and just stands there. Then Deemon pretends he does not know when Doug is here and comes in his cubicle to wait for him. He needs to stop. For someone to dislike me so much he spends an awful amount time in the vicinity of my cubicle.

01.03.18 Well Harvey Fetter keeps using his position illegally. Today I had to deal with traffic and construction on Fallen Avenue while riding the Express Bus. Traffic was halted by local Police who also has space on THE COMPANY tower in that town.

01.02.18 Harvey Fetter is still using the same old tactics to try to pressure me. This time it is having Indyah my granddaughter who is four years removed from school and in need of physical. Fetter has placed a hold on my daughter's medical insurance so she will have to pay out of pocket for all services. Currently, my daughter has been told that her daughter is unable to attend school until she has another physical. Just for the record this economic injustice tactic shall not work. Another economic tactic includes tampering with the membership balance of my mother.

On Friday, January 5, 2018, I like my coworkers to the option of working from home. My supervisor actually worked from home the day before. I forward an email to my supervisor and stating I was working from home. My supervisor sent me assignments to do. I even called in to the office and retrieve voicemail. Upon my return to work, Deemon Monstah had the secretary challenge me about my time stating I had to decide whether I was taking a vacation day or personal day. I spoke with my supervisor who stated she was going to get back to me. Deemon Monstah had the secretary charge me vacation time after I showed my supervisor the work that I did. I forwarded an email to the chief of human resources. The chief of human resources sent me an email stating she would have a meeting to resolve this issue. I guess she has not had an opportunity to meet yet. Today is March 1, 2018 and I have not heard from her. I never received and opportunity to select my time. I did not want to use a vacation day. Again, I an African American female and I am not entitled to select how I want to use my days. This was an adverse action done against as there are others who work from home all the time.

01.08.18 For the last few weeks when I go to make an electronic deposit of the Church money the machine does not want to take all the money and keep returning $2. This is another one of Fetter antics and illegal tampering with Homeland Security. So, I have to go inside of the bank to make cash deposits because every week the ATM will not accept two of the dollars given.

Hopefully, they have not changed the original Father Documents approved and signed by company Board of Directors. With illegal use of this technology and invasion of the Synapse Gap, axon, and ace they can send signals to the brain. Over the weekend I was constantly threatened about my legs and the cramp the initiated in my left foot along with reminders of leg amputation. I am looking forward to when the federal investigation of former Governor Harvey Fetter starts. The intimidation of having Ford Escalade vehicles from former

Governor Fetter follow me is not working. The Truth is coming out about this whole racist matter. While Deemon Monstah has major psychological issues and the driving force against me, please know it is Governor Fetter who has given the approval and authorization of the state wide illegal use of police brutality and racial profiling. The drug promotion for this state is a scan. Check the relations between Governor Fetter and university research scientists. This is just an umbrella to continue the illegal drug use and synapse usage.

01.08.18 Also the chemical warfare continues with the fever sore virus given to me. Electrical synapses can be converted into chemical synapses and fuse with healthy cells to cause this physical problem.

01.16.18 In 2011, when I received an unfair Performance Appraisal, I asked to have my attorney present for a meeting. I was denied the privilege of having an attorney present. On several occasions, since then, the company has scheduled meetings with me under false pretenses. They will have my supervisor call me and state she wants to speak to me under the guise of work related issue. When I arrive to her office Human Resources is there. I feel this practice is unethical and illegal. They have done this several other employees. I normally excuse myself from the meeting because any meeting with Human Resources regarding my pay or benefits my attorney should be present. In the past, they use Peg to hand you a letter to send you home or have the Senior Director for Human Resource Business Affairs to call you for a meeting and they both give you a policy devised for Rail and Bus for personnel who are on the front lines and they twist the policy to include Black Corporate employees. This way they try to force you to go to Medical for EAP. As stated in the Resolution for African Americans Development & Career Advancement this is one of their tactics using a person of color in Human Resources to attack another person of color. The purpose is to portray you as an angry Black woman.

How many pieces of the puzzle do you need before you get the clear picture of what is happening? If I never see Deemon Monstah again it will be too soon! All I receive when I do receive a response is inconsistencies in responses. What is the crime you are trying to cover that you need to obstruct justice and hide? With illegal use of Homeland Security the extraordinary access given to a person who is jealous, weak, insecure and vicious. Who focus on petty things instead dealing with itself. Welcome to my world. I have to deal with this on an ongoing basis.

The acts are outrageous chaotic governance, tumult, rambling and devastating. This explosive account of the corporate is nothing more than a dysfunctional play room for racist with power, position and money.

The corner office is filled with a nasty vile aggressive demon. Moreover, no one in the conspiracy seems to know their job in which they were hired to do or care. Incompetence is the qualification as viewed in every decision and act. The appalling view of a frightened unqualified person making decisions is so overwhelmed because they are an unprepared gang leader and cannot think straight or rational.

No one is monitoring the pattern of behavior. The illegal economic pressure that is being applied over a period of time is a very serious situation. Clearly the complicit collaboration is repeatedly done to derail investigation and interfere with the legal process. In addition to the abusive use of surveillance and violation of the privacy law, this concerted conspiracy to deny and delay justice is nothing more than high tech slavery abuse. To say that the practice is highly improper is an understatement. The tide has turned. Evil has overplayed its hand and underestimate the truth.

With some people there are more than just racial resentment going on with them. Racial resentment includes feelings of injustice. Persons with harbor racial resentment are offended by claims of racial discrimination. What happens when you have a racist that have other psychological and emotional issues?

With this change of events, vacations are used to deal with the altered personality that surfaces and takes over when he feels threatened. Deep depression sets in and exhaustion is expected. When Jennifer surfaces she is woman scorned. Jennifer wears female clothes, make-up, paints her nails, and has many wigs. When Jennifer looks into the mirror she sees a beautiful thin blonde with long hair. What a delusion! The fact is the image reveals a middle age, overweight bald man. His resume is a forgery. Without the medication, its bodily presence is weak and his speech is contemptible. Some unveilings are hideous and grotesques. To this end, part of the reason my daughter is suffering is not only because she is my daughter and assisted me. She is suffering because she is a beautiful young black woman. Deemon despises her for her age and her beauty. Because of that both she and I shall pay. This is Economic Injustice at its worst. How do I know some of these things? Deemon Monstah in his devious planning did not take some obvious things into consideration. I was moved closer to Deemon so he may keep an eye on me and be connected to my work computer to control my emails and workload. Deemon listened to my telephone conversations and viewed who came in and out of my cubicle. Deemon should have known that the door swings both ways. I was able to listen to his conversations and see who comes in out of his office. Most people think you cannot hear with the door closed with these paper-thin walls. You actually hear better when they close the door.

Chapter Six

No Boundaries & No Limits

For violence against your brother Jacob, Shame shall cover you, and you shall be cut off forever.
The Book of Obadiah verse 10 [v]

Parents Move

My parents move from Maryland to this state is an important part of this testimony as it shows Deemon Monstah crossed state lines to retaliate against my family and me. No distance is too far, no law can restrain him from lashing out at me. My parents who are in their eighties are paying for one reason only and that is because they are my parents. My parents would not know Deemon Monstah if he was standing in front them, yet he has stolen family heirlooms, money and other items from them. Items that will never be replaced and hold the type of value that he will never understand such as a handmade quilt with patchwork from my grandmother's grandmother.

Current Lawsuit Parent Move Interstate across State Lines

I wrote a letter on behalf of my parents the Starrs. Below are some excerpts from the letter. There were three movers that showed up at the Baltimore Maryland address on November 28, 2014 and packed the house. I also sent the Guaranteed & Binding Price Pledge from The Company and Dispatch Ticket Contract. Both clearly stated my father paid for additional insurance to be covered for almost $4,000. Little did we know at the time that Deemon Monstah was receiving the mail and one responding back until I noticed the incoherent writing, long responses and confused thought patterns he wrote.

On the delivery day December 12, 2014 to the address the following incidents occurred and it needs to be investigated.

1. Only one mover came to the address to unpack the truck and bring all the items in.
2. The one mover did not review the list of items with my parents nor did he check off the boxes as he brought them in.
3. The boxes were not in order and very difficult to locate all the boxes and the numbers that were supposedly to be placed on the boxes.
4. Items were broken that were in a few of the boxes.
5. The mover stated he packed the truck the night before he left Virginia and the truck sat at his home. We have no way of knowing if boxes were taken from that location.
6. Because only one mover showed up two hours past the scheduled time of arrival and was alone it took an extended length of time for him to unpack the boxes which caused a great hardship and physical fatigue to my elderly parents.
7. My parents who are almost eighty years old had to assist in moving furniture which defeats the purpose of paying for movers.

I further stated that In lieu of the above, what I am requesting since my father is showing proof that he has insurance that you bring the missing boxes which is too numerous to list or reimburse my parents for the <u>full amount of insurance</u>. If the other missing boxes are received, we will give you the list of the items that were broken for reimbursement.

1. What was the name of the driver?
2. What type of truck was issued for this move?
3. What was the truck route from the designated location of pick up until it reached my parents' home?

4. Did the driver make any stops? If so, where, when and why?
5. Did any unauthorized person board the truck? If so, where, when and why?
6. Why only supposedly one driver during a long trip that requires loading and unloading?
7. Does their tolls and gas stop correspond with their route?

I did not know at the time that my certified letters were being intercepted at the post office and the moving company never received any of my letters. I further assert that the advertising company acted as a coconspirator and diverted the delivery of my parents' items. None of the above questions was answered. I hope that during the second trial that involve former Governor Harvey Fetter that the truth comes. My parents paid for insurance of their items and to this day never received their items or their insurance money. This is such an economic injustice done to the elderly just because they were my parents. Precious family photos and heirlooms lost. While they may not be of value to anyone else some of the items taken have been in the family for generations and it was the hopes they we would be able to continue to have these items. Bowls and small tables that were hand made during slavery time from our family history are now gone. I also notice that the truck drove to Virginia before coming to this state. Virginia is out of the way which this is another piece of the puzzle as Virginia is where they stopped my daughter. I contend that the advertising company has a connection in Virginia as do the company police.

12.16.15 Deemon Monstah's latest scheme is to have my personal cell phone shut off again.

03.21.16 Today's terrorizing tactics is having my personal cell phone blacked and my work cell phone stolen.

03.21.16 The Governor has to know about this racial abuse and what these three agencies are doing.

12.20.16 as of date, the Advertising company intersected my parent's moving truck and stole items off of them. Hence, the new name of the advertising company. They paid the driver to stop and to allow them to take items off the truck. This is another Federal offense in which it was approved by former Governor Fetter. In trying to file a claim, my mail was intersected from the US Post Office, and it was Deemon that responded to all my letters. My father was entitled to full reimbursement for lost items. My father paid the additional insurance to ensure his items were covered and Deemon Nadell stole the items and the money with the help of the six company police officers and the advertising company. He robbed the elderly because they were my parents. In addition, he used the illegal money he stole to further his racist acts of having fake film shoots. Please review all the films and commercials done by the Acquisition Assets division since 2013. It will reveal the tragic story of a very sick person using their position to advance their psychotic behavior.

Passageville Patrol

I attended church on a Saturday in November and my vehicle was ticketed and towed. The reason was that my registration was supposedly expired. The fact is they stole my registration and planned to have my car ticketed and towed because it was a three-day weekend and the tow company charges daily for the tow storage of vehicle. In addition, and a lesson learned all information was in the glove department, so I have to wait and receive the other necessary documents before getting my vehicle which cost me another day. I decided to go to court so that I could share the whole story. The judge instructed the cameras to be off during my testimony. The police officer was a friend of Office Punster. The judge never let me share my testimony of what happened.

I was then made the joke and given the cynical sense of humor of Deemon to work on the Passageville Patrol Contract Agreement which coincides with what happen to me in Passageville Patrol. I am the human resource that is referenced in that contract.

05.18.16 Check Passageville Patrol Court records and investigation of officer for details

Virginia/Dallas Trip

As I share the below experience, I want to reiterate that the Dallas trip is with a company affiliate for minority employees. The Texas trip I was denied is a trip that all my white coworkers were able to attend, and I was denied that opportunity. While Deemon had a major fit over me attending the Dallas trip, he could not prevent that because it was for minorities.

08.03.16 The backlash of this aggressive hatred of me has crossed state lines into a federal offense with racial profiling by a Virginia Police Officer. In 2013, my home was broken into and my car manual for the 2010 Honda Pilot was stolen. Being that the car is mostly computerized and with these cyber pirates they have crossed state lines with this racial control. Who has granted these few Officers license to discriminate on the federal level? Please consider the collateral consequences and the magnitude of your actions.

On 07.08.16 Deputy Officer of Interstate 81 was involved in a racial profile and illegal stop. There should be a full internal investigation. My daughter was stop falsely for speeding via a computerized device (speed gun) contact made through the company police officer from list. I recommend checking Officer Punster's phone records as he previously did this in Passageville Patrol, with me and had my car towed. The purpose again for harassing my daughter is because she is my daughter. I have her on my car insurance and they want points added to her license to increase my insurance premium as vendetta against me is to have me unemployed and broke. The retaliation is because I demand equal rights in employment as my coworkers. I am being penalized for speaking up in which I will continue to do without hesitation. Officer Punster a few days back threaten me about using the US Postal system as he has done in the past tampering and actually stealing the mail to give to Deemon Monstah to respond to me instead of the actually person or entity that I was writing all of this with the blessing of Mitch Holden and Governor Fetter. Virginia is one of the toughest states to receive a speeding ticket. While it is standard for attorneys to send letters to take your case in a moving violation, my daughter received several. It was their original hopes that she would just give money away to a stranger and have fake documents and fees. However, we drove back to Virginia to the kangaroo court. We sat in court while it was intentional to have many cases unrelated to traffic combine in one court, so we would have to wait all day and listen to the nonsense. The court time was 8:30 am and we did not get seen until after 3pm.

Capt. Linden Weeke at the request of Deemon Monstah has already made arrangements to have my daughter receive points on her license. The purpose is to have her car insurance sky rocket and cause a great financial hardship. Deemon Monstah will stop at nothing and break every law conceivable just to steal money from me. Deemon Monstah has had my daughter and my car several times in hit and runs. In Deemon's demented mind, we should not have vehicles. Just because Deemon Monstah is friends with the Governor who has had his ethics called into question on several occasions, the company has allowed Deemon Monstah do whatever he wants and that includes using a select few of The Company Police, IS technology with Holden's assistance, Federal and State funds and technology. Please note that company is supporting the cause of racism by financing Deemon Monstah's illegal operation.

Cars Towed & Ticketed

12.16.15 The company police are still having their friends give my daughter tickets and also tampering with DMV electronically with daughter's license.

02.22.16 The company police are still allowed to use terroristic tactics in terrorizing my daughter with their MOU with all Police throughout the state, Court System and DMV.

02.22.16 The company police are still tampering with US Postal mail and illegal use of IRS records.

02.24.16 The company police contacted the local Police to have daughter stopped and told her that her license was suspended. The vehicle was towed and cost $417. When she went to verify the information, it was a lie. Her license was not suspended. The company police are still using illegal means of tampering with DMV to harass my family and me.

07.22.16 Another vicious attack occurred on Friday at 5pm, evening in the company parking lot of hitting my car from the back and then driver not sharing the license, insurance and registration information with a phony license plate USI CIS.

08.30.16 The new terrorizing financial tactic is to increase my car insurance with several minor car accidents. By having people hit my daughter and my car. Being that the company has access to DMV the select few manipulate data impacting my car insurance. This is one of the new institutional racism tactics using technology. They set up various technical ways to abuse their positions, company's resources and its contacts all with the Governor's approval.

10.18.16 I am following up on a false claim number against my car insurance please note the claim number and name.

11.08.16 Deemon is also attacking my daughter again. He has her followed and trying to set up scenarios to force her to park illegally, so he can have police to give her a ticket. A phony speeding ticket was given at Deemon's request via Deemon's connection with the Governor Fetter. The purpose again for cause me a financial hardship with tickets and fines.

11.07.16 illegal tampering with car keys. Car towed cost $200 cash. $30 cash stolen. Receipt for car tow stolen. Car keys replacement $289.

Now I am receiving threats about daughter receiving parking tickets and they plans of tampering with US Postal mail again. You would think Governor Fetter would have enough on his plate besides the company illegal use of Homeland Security for racial discrimination.

11.08.16 So the scam with the illegal use of technology was to divert my call to AAA on Sunday for them to use Homeland Security and sending a fake tow truck which explains why I was forced to pay cash and receipt was stolen. In addition to the statement below from a document Band Festival - Sunday, November 6, 2016 from 8am to 6pm, *"lot for practice on Sunday, November 6, 2016 from 8am to 6pm."* Deemon Monstah has a fetish with my 2010 Honda Pilot. He believes I should not have this vehicle and therefore he keeps using illegal means to have my vehicle taken away from me. From stealing money out of my bank account to false fees on the monthly payment to having the vehicle towed to having the car keys stolen to having the car not starting. Please note if this continues to happen, it is approved by Mitch Holden and Governor Fetter. Look at the connection with technology contracts, the Father Documents, the Little Rock Consulting Firm Contracts and advertising contracts and the trail will lead to former Governor Fetter. Follow the money of these transactions and they will lead to their dummy companies which Deemon Monstah and Harvey Fetter own. They are getting rich off of taxpayer's money. They are diverting state and federal funds. In addition, look at Deemon Monstah's personal life and it will explain his behavior. Why haven't Deemon had a psychological evaluation? Money laundering, commingling funds, discrimination, lies all of this takes a toll on a person as well. Look at him. Take time and a long look at Deemon today. He is showing all the signs.

11. 08.16 All Hawk-Eye systems are based on the principles of triangulation using the visual images and timing data provided by a number of high-speed video cameras located at different locations and angles around the area of play. Ask the company Police do they have the Hawk-Eye equipment and have they used it on my family and me. I received an email for a work request after being stranded with my granddaughters.

The Wee is representative of the two little African American girls ages 3 and 5 left stranded for 2 hours to stand in the cold and dark, with no cell phone and no food.
The "No Issues" were the no food and no cell phone to ensure being stranded.
The names are the little girls Indyah age 3 and Iyanna age 5.

Yes, Homeland Security at its best! Coincidence that it the email stated tow-state? The same day my keys were stolen and my car needed to be towed. I think not. Deemon Monstah has a sick mind and enjoys using email requests to inform everyone and me what he plans to do because with Mitch Holden, the select few THE COMPANY Police and Governor Fetter's approval he believes he can commit any crime he wants.

11.09.16 *The* Company's illegal use of Homeland Security left two little girls stranded their names are Indyah age 3 and Iyanna age 5. They had no food and no cell phone. The cell phone was blacked out. This is a process that is supposedly used on trains to protect commuters from bombings. The response from Leadership on this so-called mission was "We had a very successful event and no issues".

Please note: I was with my two small grand children ages 3 and 5 at the time of this crime. This is how Homeland Security is being used. Divert calls of help to AAA and have someone carry a Reverend a Grandmother and two small children across the state. Be mindful, technology was used to black out my cell phone. So, the children had not eaten since breakfast. They made me wait 2 hours before contacting me back. But I guess it is okay because we are African Americans and this is what the federal money is used to do.

11.14.16 As the saga continues please note the road construction that was scheduled during my trip to Philadelphia this weekend. I contend that this was another Governor Fetter approved conspiracy and abuse at the request of Deemon Monstah to cause back up, gridlock, and delays of innocent people. Is it a coincidence that when I plan to travel the roads are blocked, detoured or under construction. Specifically, this weekend going to Philly and traffic with the GSP. Officer Punster coordinated with Philadelphia Police and had me blocked in the parking lot. These are other Federal Investigations that needs to happen.

Racial Profiled/Stopped by Police

12.24.15 I will continue to report daily the illegal actions of Deemon Monstah and the few company police officers that practices racial profiling of the company customers on the buses. On the buses is overcrowding. Currently, about 35 people are standing and some with bags. This is another example of abuse of power and taking advantage of minorities with Bus service. On occasion, women who are pregnant and women with small children have to stand. Because of the harassment and retaliation other minorities are suffering. The 1:10 and 1:20 was late. The 1:10 came at 1:22 pm.

01.14.16 increase having local Police give daughter tickets (racial profiling);

05.19.16 Unnecessary stops of daughter's boyfriend and unnecessarily being held in Jail. THE COMPANY Police using influence to detain him as retaliation against me because he is a friend of my daughter.

Attempted Murder

03.02.16 Technology & physics had daughters' tire roll across 78. The lug nuts were removed from tire to cause accident and to delay grandson from going to school.

03.03.16 This terrorism has escalated to attempted murder. My daughter and grandson could have been killed because of the loosening of the nuts from the tire. Technology was used on my daughter's loan to accelerate the debt, delay receipt of mail and to confiscate her income tax. The violent attack has moved from me to pressure me because I am telling the truth to my daughter and grandchildren. All of this can be exposed by reviewing the technology contracts, the capability, who has access, and who gave approval of access along with a trip to Washington, DC. Who gave the company police approval to execute these terroristic tactics against my family and me?

Money Laundering

05.18.16 The Little Rock Consulting Firm funnels money through Bank of America off shore accounts for Terrorism. Investigate accounts. Check work emails requests that coincide with my mortgage being transferred from Bank of America and sold.

While Deemon Monstah has shown no remorse and believe he has no limits and no boundaries it is up to our Federal Government to intervene and show him that we as a nation do have limits of the law and when you cross the boundaries of human trafficking even in the technical and ethical realm we as a country have boundaries. If an unjust law is no law at all, a just law that is not enforced can have the same results. I am advocating let's uphold the law not just for me but also for others. How many lives do we have to lose before this is considered a serious matter?

Chapter Seven

No Exit Plan

The race is not given to the swift, nor to the strong, but to them that endure to the end.
(Ecclesiastes 9:11)[vi]

In the midst of all the staged chaos I would tell myself these words. You shall finish all of your assignments. So let it be written. So let it be done. My weapons are the pen and prayer. In all their planning they did not have an exit plan. When I walk into a room the first thing I look for is the nearest exit besides the way I entered. Today my exit or way of escape will be this book. My adversary on the hand did not have an exit plan as he planned to torment and torture me for life. With that said, I will give the structure of the institutional racism and how they the selected few were able to violate my human rights for so long.

Institutional Racism – The Structure

1. The former Governor Harvey Fetter gave approval for the illegal use of Homeland Security Conspiracy for Hate Crimes. As of date, I have not heard from his office with the information that I hand-delivered to his office and gave to his aids. Check the record and you will see they all have Federal Government Contracts. Through the former Governor Fetter they have the use of technology, funds and opportunity for Domestic Terrorism against African Americans. Harvey Fetter is a shyster lawyer who has shyster lawyer friends. Review the executive orders he had done. The committees he formed and the budgets he approved. Follow the money.

2. Jill Transzell - Chief of Staff in Executive Director's Office promoted now in Governor's Office in the Technology Division. After Governor Fetter gave the approval for the conspiracy of the Hate Crimes Jill initiated the email to me stating the request came from the Governor's Office and placed me on the Black List under guise of the film "The Black List". There is a Black List of employees that have EEO complaints or lawsuits which we are considered a risk to the current social order of institutional racism. Jill went back and forth between the company and the governor's office depending on where the heat was. Jill is just as ruthless as her male counterparts and deserves the same punishment that they receive.

3. Stan W. Scramberg – Chief, Government & External Affairs promoted to the company Chief of Staff and is the University Medical Research contact for the biological warfare tactics along with the Technology School of Engineering contact for the technical expertise of the high tech equipment. Stan's role was to use his title and position in case anyone question any request that the University Medical Research team wanted to do.

4. Holden Mitch – Chief, Information Office & Homeland Security IS Contact (Initiator of the Father Document 2012) and contact of Homeland Security Technology source in town and in the former Governor's Office. Holden Mitch uses his security clearance to run illegal checks on African Americans and their families and friends. I was told by Human Resources that Holden was no longer with The Company. The day I filed my last EEO Complaint I saw Holden Mitch in the hallway and have been seeing him in passing ever since. I am not sure why Human Resources felt the need to lie.

5. Deemon Monstah – Senior Director, Acquisition Assets (AA) (Signed The Father Document 2012) Devise and implemented conspiracy for Hate Crimes using Homeland Security and the selected team for the conspiracy pack agreement. Deemon was pivotal in his role of Senior Director using the Little Rock Consulting Firm and the Advertising Company. Deemon was the conductor leading the band for me to be the human experiment because I filed a discrimination lawsuit against him. Initially, he had an opportunity to service several of his needs. Deemon was able to use retaliation against me, make more illegal money, and elevate himself for power.

6. Nick Stelton – Director, under Deemon. Nick was a mere henchmen doing Deemon's bidding. Deemon is a coward and never does his own dirty work. Nick tripped himself up by lying during Discovery and was fired. They the select few stated it for retirement. Nick was used by Deemon as the fall guy.

7. Poe Ledesham was the Deputy Chief of The Company Police and retired. Ledesham had a scheduled retirement. The initial plan was to have me handled by Christmas of 2013 and he would retire in January of 2014. With the grace of heaven I survived the poisoning, the October and November 2013 break-ins into my home. Poe left but when in a tight squeeze the select few would reach out to him.

8. Linden Weeke – Former Police Inspector of the company and worked under the known racist Chief of Police who was fired because of losing a discrimination lawsuit. Linden Weeke wanted to show Deemon Monstah that he can take over the in Poe's absence. Linden had an office down the hall from Deemon and they would meet every day to strategize. This stop

after I reported the death of my brother and asked for an investigation. Linden was temporarily demoted from Inspector to Captain. He is now Deputy Chief.

9. Wyner Punster – Captain, Police Records and responsible for making telephone calls to other police officers to illegally stop, ticket and tow my family, friends and myself in our vehicles. Punster handled the racial profiling detail. I identified Wyner Punster as being one of the officers parked across the street from my vehicle prior to the start of the break-ins. As of date, I have received no report on the matter.

10. Fred Snackes – Captain of Police, Special Operations (Homeland Security) is not promoted to Inspector of Special Operations. Fred serves under Linden Weeke.

11. Ulysses Lefte – Police Officer under the supervision of Fred Snackes, Special Operations (Homeland Security) left company after I reported the death of my brother to the company police Internal Investigations.

12. Saul Drew – Company Police Officer Intake Officer and witness of both desk locks being broken. I do not know his whereabouts at this time.

12.21.16 With racial resentment from Deemon Monstah Holden Mitch handles the Tactical Intelligence and should be held accountable. He is liaison with Homeland Security and the company police. He is directly responsible for my personal cell phone being blacked out having the alarm continuously going off. I am still requesting a Special Investigation from Washington DC Justice Department for this abuse.

06.22.17 Today, the Domestic Terrorists are in full force with their full team. Every now and then Deemon Monstah likes to have me see his team.

The PACK

09.29.16 What is the common denominator in this terrorizing and discrimination have in common?

The DAG, The Board of Directors, The company police, the university medical research team, the District Attorney's Office, the judge that tried my first case along with Deemon Monstah and his team (Little Rock Consulting Firm & The Advertising Agency) all have in common? The Answer is the Governor. How can he not know what is going on in his own state which he ultimately signs off on and approve a budget for to happen? Homeland Security reports to him in the state. The Governor would know about domestic terrorists unless, he is a part of it. Follow the Money. Check Bank accounts and phony companies.

The Grinch That Stole Christmas

12.16.15 Tammy Sweets was set up by Deemon Monstah and he took her money. Tammy Sweets was staying with me. Tammy was supposed to save up her money and get on her feet financially. Tammy in her desperation to make a little extra took on a part time job of wrapping gifts. The way it was supposed to work is the company would send her gifts to wrap. The company would supply the gift-wrapping items and the postage to mail the gift. For each gift she mails she would get a check based on the size of the gift. The first three gifts were small in size and very expensive gifts such as a cell phone, watch, and jewelry. We assumed it was a test. Then the gifts got bigger and heavier. What I did not know was after the third gift was that Tammy was paying out of pocket. Tammy started to get the runaround when she started to call. By the time she shared with me that she did not receive her checks from the last three gifts I figured okay it was a scam. She later informed me because they were giving her the runaround she was paying out of pocket to mail the gifts because they assured her she was going to get paid. Tammy mailed three gifts and paid out of pocket the last gift were weights for a person who worked out in a gym. The whole purpose of Tammy staying with me was to make extra money to get on her feet and to have a nice Christmas for her and her son. Tammy told me she was paying out of pocket; I told her it was a scam. Deemon got his wish as he listens to my telephone calls and read my emails and texts. Needless to say, Tammy did not have money to give me for staying with me, nor did she have money for her son for Christmas.

This is the type of evilness that my family and friend have had to endure over the past ten years. This also speaks to the type of creature Deemon Monstah really is. All of this was done so that a friend of mine would not give me a few dollars for staying with me. Tammy did go to the township police and filed a report. As I already know it was a phony company with a website and 1.800 number. She filed a police report for fraud on gift wrapping scam. I guarantee it leads to Deemon Monstah.

Look at all the technology contracts, who signed by parties and with are they purpose and benefits. No one is viewing with these contracts and seeing what these scientists are allowed to do. They took the oath to preserve life not to destroy it. Why is the Governor's Office allowing these so-called doctors perform the "Tuskegee Experiments" on African Americans under the guise of Homeland Security Anti-terrorism when they are one actually using science and technology to terrorize?

05.12.17 Today's threat is that I will fall. Again, all credit goes to former Governor Harvey Fetter for his authorization and approval. While Deemon is the agitator and initiator, he cannot do anything without Fetter's approval. When the State is ready to go public on the news with the Homeland Security abuse, Fetter's Executive Orders and how all this ties into the Crossover Tunnel delays, I am ready. The only thing stopping me at this point is when I try to connect to the news the illegal tampering to my technology happens. Meanwhile, evidence is accumulating all thanks to Deemon Monstah's involvement with sending threatening emails and texts to me which actually reveals the Father Document plan with Technology, the Healthcare, Medications/Drugs, Executive Orders, and the statewide legislation.

05.11.17 I am still receiving threats of breaking into my home or setting my home on fire. With the communication technology and synapse gaps even in cats he can and has shown me that he can have it squirm around uncontrollably. I was able to sell six tickets for a luncheon in which I was receiving a humanitarian award. Deemon Monstah literally had a fit. My oldest granddaughter was with me when we saw a cat go into an erratic frenzy in the middle of the street.

Now, upon my return to work is the ongoing threats of being sent to EAP where they want to me see their doctor to prescribe medication. And now, the constant threat of going to Human Resources and signing some illegal document for one million dollars and a minimal increase in pay of what I asked for 10 years ago. What would be the benefit of this and they are still allowed to torture via technology and commit felonies. Then send messages stating I have no proof because no one reviews the list of technology they have for Homeland Security.

All of the below are directives, approvals and authorization of former Governor Fetter as everyone now know the relationship between his push for medical services and drug treatment is part of a master plan in which he caused and the direct relationship with cell towers and human cells. I <u>shall not</u> give in or submit to Domestic Racist Terrorists. I will not enter into any type of agreement with any of these criminals. Let's be crystal clear The Federal Government needs to intervene. These monsters are out of control. I <u>shall not sign</u> any document with these lying unethical thieves.

The Runaround/The Stall

Within the runaround and stall they believe they have a solution which in essence more tragic then their original plan. First, it is the economic squeeze play to force me to do what they want. They being the selected few have access to your financial records and utilities so they continuously change due dates, amounts, increase the interest delay and stop payments, and hold checks. All in this is done in the hopes of bringing you to financial ruins. I openly admit I have made the sacrifice of eating peanut butter and jelly, walking as much as possible to save gas, and I do not shop. I have cut my hair into a short afro to keep hair maintenance to a minimum. They have destroyed my house with the break-ins. Some of the damage done is banister rails broken, the water leak from the second-floor bathroom to the living room, the screen to the front door destroyed. There is no need in replacing or fixing anything at this time because they will only break in again to do more damage. I am hoping that after this is revealed I can start to rebuild and piece my life back together.

They have done the following:

05.09.16 This abuse with the use of Homeland Security has stolen my human dignity and violated my civil rights. This abused of the 4th Amendment rights of a human being is because of greed and racism. I am still being threatened with Identity Theft and the select few sharing my information via the illegal use of federal technology given for Homeland Security.

08.14.17 I am receiving still receiving continuous harassment with 1-800 numbers and other numbers to set up meetings and have a discussion. The correct process and procedure is to schedule an appointment on the work calendar manager stating the purpose of meeting and state who is attending. I will continue to ignore the telephone harassment and document this unprofessional, unethical illegal behavior that the company continues to reward by allowing the company Police and Management conduct themselves under the orders and authorization of former Governor

Fetter. Zero tolerance for discrimination and harassment is an ongoing joke.

Physical Evidence Not Investigated

My desk at work was broken into and personal file cabinet that I purchased the lock was sawed and broken as well. I filed a police report and had the company police officer view this for his self. This information never made it to court. The police reports, the performance reviews, my job description stating I handle telecommunication projects, the white powder found at my desk, the list of questions for human resources sending me home from EAP, and a copy of the internal affairs police report of the investigation of my brother's death never made it to court. The senior director took me by the arm and escorted me to the human resources conference room. No mention of this behavior was introduced at the trial. A big piece of evidence was the police officer who issued the recommendation to send me to Medical is the same police officer accused of having something to do with my brother's death and illegal use of Homeland Security Technology.

I was placed in the hospital on Friday, October 2013 and released on Saturday, October 2013 because I was given some type of poison at work and food was tampered with in my desk drawer. I have been carrying my bag with me ever since. Deemon wanted to imply that something was wrong me. Deemon prompted coworkers to inquire of me why I carry my bags around knowing full well he poisoned me.

This morning on my birthday there was a substance that looked like artificial ashes found on my desk this morning. I ignored it and wiped it off. Upon my return from lunch the substance was found again. I know Deemon Monstah has a fetish with fire and as in the past threaten to burn my house and the church I attended down. I am taking this as another threat from to burn my house down. While I know Deemon Monstah is not here his associates Captain Linden Weeke in the company police is.

The Unanswered Ethical Questions
(Constitutional & Human Rights)

I too am a part of America!

12.16.15 Deemon Monstah is bi-polar and because of his illness Deemon is insecure, weak and scared. Deemon Monstah has done some heinous, vicious cruel things to my family, friends and me. I will have no problem testifying at the Congressional hearing of the technological experiments and abuse because of racism that a handful of corrupted company Police Officers, Deemon Monstah and Holden Mitch have been allowed to do under the Board Approved Father Document 2012 for Communications. Does the Board of Directors at the company really know what they have approved?

11/10/15. Has anyone done a psychological evaluation on Deemon Monstah?

03.24.16 Where is the written report for the in-house terrorism of the company police officers? Who is the Homeland Security contact in DC that allowed all of this to continue?

04.07.16 As the abuse continues to heighten why not concentrate on the internal audit of Little Rock Consulting Firm, its old contracts, and the kickbacks that are received from them. Who is actually responsible for the contract and lease compliance? Why did we remove 3 permanent employees and replace them with 5 contract employees? Was this done to hide the cover up in the money funneled from the contracts? I strongly suggest you do an investigation into the individuals' bank accounts and you will see the money. Follow the money trail.

08.02.16 The latest dreadful diabolical maneuver is to have my home computer shut down and tamper with my personal cell phone to try to force me to utilize work computer as grounds to fire me. They are allowed to use federal funds for equipment and technology for Homeland Security to manipulate illegal endeavors. To serve and protect Who? Themselves. They are not preventing crimes they are creating them.

08.02.16 My Home computer and printer still not working at home due to the abuse of technology being allowed to be used by a select few the company police. Now the threat is to send me to medical again. Last time I was sent to Medical was because of the Board Approved Father Document scandal with Telecommunications in 2012. This time the threat of sending me to medical is because of continued retaliation and to remove me from work. Please note the attempt is for me to see their University Scientist owned doctor to have his own diagnoses. Keep in mind that University has technical uses from the Father Documents as well. Please interview Holden Mitch and his contact at Homeland Security to substantiate the truth. These are simple questions that should be answered. Please note my log is limited to a specific list of people that have been allowed to control and manipulate the system. Before any one sends me to medical, send Deemon Monstah first.

1. Does the company police have the technology or not?
2. Is the company police using the technology or not?
3. What technology does the company have? The investigation is not that difficult.
4. For this to go on this long does it mean the former Governor's Office approves of using technology to terrorize people?
5. Why no investigation report given to complainant? Was it because no investigation or report done? That would mean the truth would be in writing.
6. This technology should be removed from THE COMPANY Police because of their abuse of it.

7. If Homeland Security is federally funded, there should be no discrimination.

Review each statement in the terrorized list and match the federally funded technology to it.

08.01.16 Company Police still using Homeland Security to deny me access to my home personal computer and printer.

08.01.16 The Pencil Whip Strategy continues with the phony assignments and tedious tasks.

08.03.16 The backlash of this aggressive hatred of me has crossed state lines into federal offenses with racial profiling by a Virginia Police Officer. In 2013, my home was broken into and my car manual for the 2010 Honda Pilot was stolen. Being that the car is mostly computerized and with these cyber pirates they have crossed state lines with this racial control. Who has granted these few police officers license to discriminate on the federal level? Please consider the collateral consequences and the magnitude of your actions.

08.03.16 The virulent racism continues with diverting my personal cell phone call and personal email to their number pretending to be a member of my denomination staff. There is no "equal protection of the law" concerning the fraudulent abuse that a corrupted few is allowed to do. In addition to the stealing of my Minority Professional Organization membership payment out of the US Postal mail and removing my entry of being nominating from Minority Professional Organization online. I am still receiving the threat of IRS investigation. This abuse of the technology system guarantees discriminatory results. If you want proof read the Father Documents 2012 and follow the funds in Capital Planning. Those of you in the company that do nothing make you an accessory to cybercrimes. Having a blind eye and pretending not to know will be no excuse.

08.05.16 While being stigmatized and singled out for protecting my belongings. My Fourth Amendment rights have been violated from unreasonable searches and the right to be secure in my person and papers. Please be reminded I have never been given a search warrant for these searches. The reason I carry both my purse and my workbag is because my desk and personal file cabinet was broken into. Capt. Punster and Officer Drew took reports of the incidents. Officer Drew inspected the work area and noted the lock was broken on my drawer and personal file cabinet. As of date, no written report had been given to me as an employee who filed a report of theft. While I thought they were only looking for files, I left my lunch and to my surprised I was poison and went to the emergency room. From that point on I carry my belongings. This is being noted because of the new threat of them taking my purse and workbag from me. I receive threats of having my bag snatched.

08.30.16 Have anyone looked at the medical records especially of Deemon Monstah? Have anyone seen any police investigation report into any of the allegations? Has anyone checked Capital Planning for how the Federal and Homeland Security funds are being spent? Has anyone reviewed who has given authorization for use of equipment from Homeland Security on employees? Has anyone reviewed the Communications Father Document of 2012?

10.18.16 I just received a voicemail message with my social security number as the return call. These are the type of threats I receive prior to some illegal activity being done such as Identity Theft with my social security number.

Has anyone reviewed the psychological records of the people involved in this matter and the medications they are taking? I wonder why the constant threat of sending me to medical. I realize that some people like to put on you what is wrong with them.

03.31.17 With the former Governor's current approval as they have done in the past is place in the computer my daughter's driving license is suspended. Then when we get there it states it was an error. With the biological warfare and the use of technology from University Medical Research my daughter had to go to the Emergency room. The doctors on staff claimed she has a unique virus. Again, displaying blatant abuse of technology to try and bully me at Deemon's request to meet with them illegally.

Please explain why the former Commissioner of Transportation, the former Governor and the former Director of Homeland Security in this state is not concern with this type of abuse and terrorism when it has been brought to their attention.

One of the reasons for the runaround and the stall is this Pack (the select few) had no Exit Plan. Instead of ending this tragic fiasco, the select few under the leadership of Deemon Monstah kept escalating the evil deeds in the hopes that I would surrender. This was the purpose of the economic injustice bombardment on all levels. I should be broken by this point. The statement is true what does not break you will make you stronger. I found an inner strength that I did not know I had.

My Recommendation

04.07.16 Again, I recommend a Congressional Hearing in Washington, DC of the fraud and abuse that is allowed to continue with federal funds and technology. It is blatantly obvious that the company police and the company Information Technology (IT) cannot handle the federal funds given and the technology as they are abusing the system. Please know I shall testify as to how the company police and IT used federal funds to promote discrimination and other racial injustices and the company did nothing to stop it. This should be and will become public knowledge. The public should know what is going on here and how their money is being spent to support racial discrimination, abuse and other injustices.

During the Discovery process in my discrimination lawsuit Deemon Monstah made several recommendations for me to be fired despite my outstanding record prior to his arrival to this company. Today, I am making the same recommendation of him that he be fired for all the illegal activity done to my family and me.

- What measures are in place to prevent these heinous crimes from happening again to other minorities?

- What the state needs is for the Federal Justice Department to come in and investigate their mishandling of federal funds and the technology that they have been entrusted to use. Following the Federal Investigation the Federal Attorney General should assign a Special Prosecutor for the heinous crimes these people have committed.

My civic rights are being violating as I write this book is a blatant disregard and failure to comply with policy and procedure including the investigation of their own police and civil rights division.

My Plea For Federal Intervention

My cubicle became a war room before I saw the movie since I was being bombarded with negativity and insults on a daily basis. I would place Scripture in designated locations in my cubicle as words of inspiration and encouragement. With the daily attacks of racial discrimination, constant threats, the retaliation using Homeland Security technology, and the cyberbullying I have pressed my way to this point.

The guidance I offer from this book is your state of mind

and spirituality plays an important role. When you decide to take on the challenge of fighting for your freedom and those others in a similar plight, you must be spiritually and psychologically prepared. One of the daily challenges I faced was why. Why am I selected to be harassed, ridiculed and assaulted? As I sat and thought, I challenged the elite. Every day, I showed up for work I was a living witness that they were defeated. The goal was for me to be fired, broke and broken. This is why the illegal tampering with my finances and bills are crucial to them. Money is their god. Ruthless power is their temple and the financial report is the sacred book. The purpose of the book is to tell the truth of my personal experience and to enlighten the public. I know I am not the only one in this struggle. It is my hopes that I have further the cause of freedom and justice. If it is only one step it is a one step in the right direction. The benefits of this book are it gives a voice to the voiceless, a face to the faceless, and it will make someone be accountable. While I have a sleuth of evidence, it is difficult to share without giving away the real culprits and company. Again, this substantiates why we need federal intervention.

While the company denied these occurrences of oppressive acts, the fact remains, African American women with Master degrees with over 10 years of service are sent to EAP. When you challenge the structural racism or the bias institution you are placed on a (Performance Improvement File) PIF or fired while white males come in and take positions of managers in the company with no experience in that position. This is the truth look at the statistics. You can track a white male career and that of an African American with the same experience. The white male will end in five years at minimum a director; an African American if lucky will have a staff position or a low-level manager position. At a quick glance the Board of Directors all white males except for one female and in the photo you would not know she was not white. At this company, in terms of people of color, there are three people at Chief level, four people at Senior Director level, five people at Director level, and eleven people at manager level most are low level managers not making comparable to their white counterparts. This is from a company that has over 13,000 employees.

During October 2013 through December 2013 I was literally afraid to stay in my home due to the massive break-ins and the vandalism that was happening. The atrocities of racial oppression and human suffering had climaxed because I have filed a lawsuit May 18, 2013. I had raised questions in the EEO complaints that were never addressed, accumulated documentation, noted discrepancies, highlighted glaring contradictions and referenced corporate policy that was not adhered to or followed. Therefore, direct action in their view had to been taken against me for bringing their racism to the spotlight. Memorandums and emails were changed. My documents were stolen. They broke into my home, stole my originals and replace their versions in my home copies. They left no stone unturned.

I was at war and I did not know it. I thought that once the lawsuit was brought against them that this would bring things to a halt. Instead the hatred rose, the goal was that I never see the light of day in the courtroom and if I did I would have nothing to show. To ensure that they did jury tampering and the judge selected. I was naïve and unsuspecting in thinking that the system would work outside the company. I had no idea with former Governor's involvement this was an uphill battle.

Because this was a discrimination lawsuit they needed to balance what they called the racialized rhetoric with my mental capacity. The goal was she is crazy. She has to be crazy to want to go up against us an institution. They did not have to answer to the law because they were the law. It was all for one and one for all the passionate name of the **PACK**.

I reported the illegal use of license plates. I noticed that they would duplicate company license plates and put on private vehicles while they follow me around town. As of date, I have received no response pertaining to that matter.

What they could not figure out in all their doing was how she held on so long. They hit me with their best shots. Tampered with the 401l k, student loan, military pension, EZ Pass, stole jewelry and other items of value from my home. Tampered with the moving truck of my parents move and then denied my parents the insurance money. Confiscated my daughter's income tax and took her student loan. The select few stole the car manual out of my home and the car quick reference book out of vehicle to control the features on my car. The other day I walked outside and my car was started. The company police wanted to show me what they can do with their technology. I recommend that if you plan to take on this fight you plan to fight until the end.

Deemon never stated I was a bad employee or that I did not know my job. As Senior Director he never addressed the reason for wanting to fire me during the disposition. While I find it difficult to write about myself, I am an excellent employee that was progressively moving ahead in the company working nights, weekends, and holidays while attending school. I volunteered for various events and services and was due a promotion comparable to my coworkers. If you check the records I worked the longest, have the most degrees, and the most experience outside of other employee who also is an African and has the lowest paid managerial job in the department. I have managed to obtain other positions outside of the work such State Coordinator, serving on Executive Boards and being President but yet, I can obtain a managerial position comparable to my gifts, skills and talents. Because of a select few racist men, my life has been shipwrecked. In using that analogy of being shipwrecked this book is my note that I am placing in the bottle asking for help in the hopes that some Federal representative will find this note and intervene on my behalf. Help!

I recommend you keep good notes and document everything. In earlier chronological notes, I can you tell you what the culprits were wearing when certain happened. In addition to documenting make copies and put them in various places outside of your home. I have family friends holding documents and they do not even know what they are holding. Now with cell phones take photos and record conversations. While the conversation may not be admissible in court it can assist your attorney in his questions and discovery. I recommend having witnesses even though they may decline to testify. For example, I was called into my former supervisor's office. I had another employee walk with me to the door and they saw who was in the office. They decline to be a witness, but they know whom they saw. In the office were my former supervisor and human resources and others in the office. Therefore, I was justified to decline a meeting that was called under false circumstances.

For those who do not have a Supreme Being to worship, I recommend that you find your faith. What kept me and is keeping me is my faith in the all-knowing awesome Lord. I am Christian and I believe in the Lord and Savior Jesus Christ. There is no way I could have lasted this long without my faith to sustain me. I am most thankful to the Holy Spirit for leading and guiding me. I realize this book is not the end but the beginning. It is the end to suffering in silence. It is also the beginning of the Truth being told. They have been exposed and hopefully a federal investigation will take place. Confidently, it is the beginning to having monitoring and supervision over those who have been given the use and access of Homeland Security.

This book for some may find it appalling and others unrealistic. But I have learned that the truth is the truth. I welcome the challenge of anyone that contests this truth. This is simple ask the questions and answer the questions.

Instead of hiding behind the guise that she is crazy answer the question. Besides the threats, I keep hearing this is complicated. I have to disagree. It was not complicated when they sat down and plotted this conspiracy. It was not complicated when they violated the law and my personal property. Now that the truth is surfacing it is complicated. If I was a white female and this happened would it be complicated. A life is a life. My life has value. What is complicated about telling the truth? The other lie I hear continuously is this is going to impact people's lives. Again, what about my life? Did they not take into consideration that they are committing crimes and at some point there are consequences and repercussions for our actions? When do they own up to what they did? What about the impact of my life? What about the loss of my brother's life?

While they had money, power and position all I had was prayer and an ink pen. I drove to the Justice Department in Washington, DC to speak to someone about the Homeland Security abuse in this state, but I was blocked at the request of the company police inspector here. The police officers were waiting for me and they even knew my name. I traveled to Washington, D. C. twice. This is why I am pleading for help in this matter because you cannot trust the select few to govern themselves.

I understand that each state will probably want to have its own safe haven where people can file a complaint. I am leery of any state agency because of my personal experience. I went to the former Governor's office and he did nothing. I later found out he did nothing because he was the leader. I believe it is difficult to be neutral when it is in your own back yard.

Some Specifics Federal Necessities

There should be Federal and state compliance of funding; full transparency of the checks and balance concern; a safe haven for people that are victims of the Homeland Security Abuse. If your state is abusing the use of Homeland Security you should be able to physically go to Washington DC and file a complaint.

Remember the abusers have access to the emails and telephone you should be able to walk in a safe haven in Washington, DC to inform them. Every compliant should be taken seriously.

The Federal Government should send a special investigator for an independent investigation to verify whether allegation is true. What will be the ethical checks and balances for allowing someone to use these resources? Currently, you have people with special security access given authority as will. Are there any checks and balances just because one has special security access? For example, just because a person is an IT CFO it does not give them right to have access to my financial records, telephone calls and alike for no reason just because they hold a title and the special security. There needs to be a **Friend Ethic**. Just because your friend call and ask you do them a favor concerning Homeland Security there should still be a process and a procedure. No more Friends doing favors. Effective immediately, the **Friend Ethic** should be put in place.

I realize I am pressing the institution to compliance as an administrator this is what I do. There are three primary indicators of good practice:

1. **Values** – the values of people you are giving Homeland Security need to be check.

2. **Acting Justly** – While some may have the values they crack under pressure when friends ask them to do them a favor. This is why you put the **Friend Ethic** in place. If they are unable to act justly on their own the can lead on the **Friend Ethic** that everyone who has access to Homeland Security shall sign.

3. **Economics** – If there are no consequences and no repercussions there is really no law. These people are spending Federal tax dollars to break the law. We are paying for them to abuse me in addition to getting paid on company time. Most of the crimes they committed were

done on company time. All of the resources were compliments of the United States government. I strongly urge that someone add this up and make the select few pay back every single penny that they stole both from me and the federal government. They have the money just check the dummy accounts for the off-shore drilling. Please note this is in addition to any time in federal prison they will need to serve for the criminal acts.

The end goal is Accountability, Compliance and Transparency (ACT). In order to have this you have to maintain accurate records. This is a good time for everyone to rethink what he or she is doing and why. Since the ACT, the federal government needs to step in and ACT. We as a nation have a standard to live up to and a Constitution to uphold.

In closing I propose a meeting with federal officials from Washington, D.C. and representation from the state concerning Homeland Security procedures to discuss plans and strategies for policing the personnel who have use this technology. This meeting needs to take place in Washington, DC. There should be ways and means to address this on a national level and to create a network of protection for our families. Ten years of invasion of privacy is too long.

In terms of the institutional racism, this can be reviewed on the state level but without federal enforcement of the law it is a waste of time. I cannot emphasize enough that people cannot govern themselves when giving this type of access and power. It is true power corrupts. **As evidenced, police cannot police themselves nor can they handle the power and authority given them to protect the state. The former Governor gave the approval. Who checks the Governor's control?**

If the federal government would honor its policies and stop funding the state entities that have violations and evidence of a racist system, structure and acts this would lower the lawsuits and bring institutional racism to a minimum as we cannot monitor peoples' heart.

In retelling my story, I hope to change lives. I am increasingly aware of the crucial role my voice plays in this racist patriarchal institutional structure. I know my story covers an array of issues from the history of a black woman, the psychology of sick demented evil person and politics of the aftermath once the truth is now revealed. In today's workplace you will have a multilayered, multifunctional organization using technology. Who governs the CFO or IT? Who oversees his security clearance and who can he share your personal information? I encourage everyone to tell their stories and give voice to who they are and what has happened to them. The impacts of this tragic experience will linger with me for a long time. I pray daily for immediate relief. As I close this chapter and end this book I close with a quote from Albert Einstein.

No problem can be solved on the same level of thinking that created it.

On September 7, 2017, I filed Civil Lawsuit against former Governor Harvey Fetter. In this complaint, I stated that Harvey Fetter authorized the order and gave approval for illegal use of Homeland Security equipment and biological warfare to be used against me because I am an Acquisition Asset Analyst Associate (AAAA) who oversees the administration of outside carriers for telecommunication licenses and agreement. The evidence submitted was the use of the Hawkeye technology dated November 6, 2016. In addition, there is capability of cognitive experiments. If experiments are done without consent it is invasion of privacy. Please review Resolution for African Americans Development & Career Advancement pages 23-24 as supported materials and the former Governor's Executive Order. Review the report from the Commission formed from the former Governor's Executive Order. Where are the funds? As of March 2, 2018 there has been no response.

Acknowledgements

I want to thank my Lord and Savior for sustaining me through this horrible ordeal. I thank and acknowledge the presence of the Holy Spirit leading and protecting me. I thank my parents who love me and gave me their support. I thank my children and grandchildren for the sacrifice they made in the last ten years with the hell we have been through and yet survived. I thank everyone who has offered a kind word, thought or deed to me. I thank those who took the time to read my book before having it published for their input even though some of your edits were stolen from me. To my very best friend who never left my side and believed in me even when it seemed unbelievable. I acknowledge you and thank you!

Endnotes

---

[i] Chapter One
Macready, William Charles The Pen is Mightier than the sword
https://en.wikipedia.org/wiki/The_pen_is_mightier_than_the_sword (February 20, 2018)

[ii] Chapter Two
For his letters, say they, are weighty and powerful…
II Corinthians 10:10
The New King James Version Bible published by HarperCollins

[iii] Chapter Three "Give a man a mask and he'll tell you the truth." Ocsar Wilde
Brainyquotes.com (April 9, 2018)

[iv] Chapter Four
I will open my mouth in parables;
I will utter things kept secret
from the foundation of the world.
Matthew 13:34-35 NKJV[iii]
The New King James Version Bible published by HarperCollins

[v] Chapter Five
We can have democracy in this country,
or we can have great wealth concentrated
in the hands of a few,
but we can't have both.

https://www.huffingtonpost.com/peter-dreier/a-century-ago-louis-brand_b_9095998.html

[vi] Chapter Six
For violence against your brother Jacob, Shame shall cover you, and you shall be cut off forever.
The Book of Obadiah verse
The New King James Version Bible published by HarperCollins.

[vii] Chapter Seven
The race is not given to the swift, nor to the strong, but to them that endure to the end.
(Ecclesiastes 9:11)[vi]
The New King James Version Bible published by HarperCollins.

www.ingramcontent.com/pod-product-compliance
Lightning Source LLC
Chambersburg PA
CBHW052255220526
45471CB00001B/350